CELTIC MYSTERIES

The Illustrated Library of SACRED IMAGINATION

General Editor: Jill Purce

John Sharkey

celtic mysteries

The ancient religion

with 117 illustrations, 24 in colour

CROSSROAD · NEW YORK

For Jane, Kate, Gann
and all the children of
the sun

In this series the images and symbols of the
spiritual journey are explored in word and
picture, colour and form. Ancient knowledge,
eternal myth and lost traditions become a new
resource for the human venture. Some of today's
most important religious authors undertake
vision quests and discover authentic sources of
enlightenment and wholeness in oft forgotten
ways. This series constantly and directly points
the spiritually thirsty seeker to the sacred well of
the soul. For there in the heart dwells the creative
imagination. Art and architecture, nature
patterns and life cycles, mystics and their
discoveries become the key to contemplative
living.

© John Sharkey 1975

Reprinted 1981

The Crossroad Publishing Company
18 East 41st Street, New York, NY 10017

Library of Congress Catalog Card Number
81–66808

Printed in Singapore

The Ancient Religion

The central mystery of the Celtic religion, and the ceremonial rituals which embodied its essence, will always be elusive. For many the Celtic mystique, with its romantic emphasis on the fairy and the spirit-world, has obscured the spirituality of these warrior peoples and the fact that they even had a religion. The ancient oral tradition that perpetuated the laws, legends and tribal teachings, through the trained memories of a group of poets and priests, made the act of writing unnecessary. And, much like the prohibitions laid on the Celtic warrior heroes, which predestined their lives and actions, the taboo on writing continued as long as the old religion lasted.

The earliest remnants of Celtic culture in Central Europe are usually dated between 800 and 450 BC and assigned to the Hallstatt culture, after the metal artifacts found in a cemetery at Hallstatt in Austria, a centre for salt and copper mining. The later Celtic phase, the La Tène, named after a village site in Switzerland, continued in Continental Europe until Roman times. The style of ornament associated with the La Tène culture, with its wild, imaginative but formalized decoration of floral patterns and abstract symbols, was still the dominant characteristic of Celtic metalwork, stonecarving and manuscript illumination in Britain and Ireland a thousand years later.

The Celts emerged from the Rhinelands of Central Europe as a distinctive group of clans or tribes between 1000 and 500 BC. Their language, religion, social organization and customs were different from those in the Mediterranean south, or further east by the Danube. In general the Celts seem to have many affinities with Indo-European warrior groups who had overrun the Indus Valley civilizations a millennium or so earlier. A number of archaic linguistic forms, such as *raja*, king (Latin *rex*, Irish *rí* and

Gallic -*rix*) or *rigu*, queen, as well as many others connected with sacred customs and social organizations, are shared by Indo-European languages in Asia and Europe. Cultural affinities between the Celts and India can be also traced in the animal rituals in which the spirit of the new king or queen is rendered incarnate with that of a bull or horse; in the act of fasting to gain recognition for a grievance; in the position of women and the fact they were accorded parity with men (Boadicea in Britain and the legendary Maeve in Ireland) in the warrior class; in metric forms, which in the *Rig Veda*, oldest and most important of the sacred books, are similar to some early Irish and Welsh verse; and in the close relationship between teacher and pupil which is still such a feature of Indian religious life and which was an essential part of the Celtic oral tradition.

Oral transmission was an entertaining and well-perfected method of imparting all the nuances of important events within the life of the tribe. Woven into the tales, for easy rendition and remembering, were the ritual themes that revolved around the gods: the act of naming, the oracle-stone that screamed during the inauguration of a new king, the divine twins, and the heroic warrior. The constant metamorphoses of these motifs, and the easy intermingling of physical and supernatural realms, made the world of the Celtic imagination tangible through thousands of years of story-telling. In the tales, divine beings could shift from supernatural powers to human vulnerability and back without even offending the Christian susceptibilities of the scribes who eventually recorded the legends. No matter how extraordinary the deities were, they were still subject to the rhythms of this life and the demands of a particular locale. Each province or area had its sacred place that was the centre of its world; and the name of the place showed the relationship between earth and sky, the tribe and its divinity.

Much like the mystery of the inland Maya temples or the Easter Island stone heads, in our time, the effect on the Celtic sensibility of having to live among so many stone memorials of a bygone race, who appeared to have simply abandoned their temples and disappeared, is unimaginable. The prime function of myth is to explain the inexplicable. This is an undercurrent in the constant repetition and mingling of gods, goddesses and heroes around a specific ancient site or temple. The use of the sacred centre underlies its traditional appeal as a regular meeting-place and also a mythical arena where momentous events could be shifted into the ever-present time-scale of the poem and the story.

Explanations of such phenomena are always in terms of deep psychic need. In common with most nomadic tribes, the Celts on their wanderings through Europe had no pantheon of gods but were at one with the elements and the Great Spirit. Wherever they settled, their poets and seers commingled local deities with others from Greek and Asian legends, suitably altered, to do battle against their own almost human warrior heroes; so all the ancient gods and the residue of rites and folklore connected with them became part of an ancestral dream-world that was essentially Celtic.

This poetic and comprehensive viewpoint, to which the prosaic, scientific approach of archaeology is simply irrelevant, led the Celts to regard the earthworks, with their obvious aura of supernatural power, as the dwelling-place of the beings of the Otherworld which the Irish called the Sidh. The Sidh embodies the half-way state, between one world and the next, which is a vital theme of Celtic art and myth. The sacred places have retained their numinous quality down to the present. Their supernatural inhabitants, also known as the Sidh, and said to be of two kinds – the tall shining ones and the opalescents lit from within – were rarely encountered because of the impurities of the world. With the coming of Christianity they dwindled in every sense, living on in the in-between state to become the fairies, leprechauns and banshees of folklore. Their psychic reality was never wholly lost, and the comic terrors of fairy-tales and ghost stories conceal a remnant of ancient religious awe.

The Triple Goddess

The recognition of water as the first principle and source of all life to those who move over the land, dependent on its bounty for food and sustenance, is reflected in the dedication of the main river sources of Western Europe as sanctuaries to the Celtic fertility goddess. This dedication, remembered in Celtic place-names, is borne out by the large number of votive offerings – figures, skulls, precious metals, weapons and domestic objects – that have been recovered from rivers and well sanctuaries throughout Europe. The Marne had its name from the Matronae, the three Divine Mothers, and the Seine from Sequana, goddess of its source. During 1964, excavations at this sanctuary revealed nearly two hundred pieces of wood-carving, including many complete figure offerings, which showed that it was in use as a healing centre into the Roman period. The name of the Rhine is Celtic, and its eastern tributaries have Celtic names: Neckar, Main, Lahn, Ruhr and Lippe. In Britain, the Severn was named after Sabrina, and the Clyde after the goddess Clóta, Divine Cleanser, recalling the legends of the 'Hag of the Ford' – a goddess of death usually encountered by the doomed hero who knows the end is near when he sees her washing his blood-stained clothes.

The river or stream is a living expression of the Earth Mother, but this does not in itself make the waters sacred. It is a special combination of different mineral, vegetable and ethereal properties, emanating from certain springs at particular times of day or of the lunar phase, that create the regenerative powers. Every sacred spot had its guardian spirit who tended it, observed the daily rites with proper ceremony, and could materialize as cat, bird or fish, whatever form was most pleasing to the goddess – even as a hideous hag or beautiful being, depending upon the circumstance or disposition of an intruder or visitor.

Such places were womb-openings of the Earth Mother, who was invoked under many different names and aspects. There are numerous Gallo-Roman inscriptions to the Matronae, the Mother pictured as a triad – a recurrent pattern in Celtic art and literature – carrying infants, cornucopias and baskets of fruit. Another popular manifestation was Epona, usually shown on a horse and sometimes with a foal, who may have been the origin of the Lady Godiva story and other folk legends related to the horse.

The goddess is bountiful but also merciless. The moon, with its mysterious power over the tidal waters and the regular flow of menstrual blood, is the centre of a universal set of symbols; she presides over night rituals connected with such animals as the cat, the snake and the wolf. In Greek legend, as in Celtic, it is identified with the triple goddess who presides over birth, life and death: the triad of maiden, bride and crone, Morrígan, Macha and Badh in Ireland, Persephone, Demeter and Hecate in Greece. The ancient Gauls, whose theology disappeared with their oral tradition, have left nameless double- and triple-headed figures which irresistibly suggest recurrent Celtic symbols: the ambiguous facing-both-ways state, and the cyclic nature of the triad.

The characteristic manifestation of the devouring-mother aspect of the goddess in Celtic symbolism – and analogous to the bloody Kali of the Hindus or the Coatlícue of the Aztecs – is graphically illustrated by the stone effigies known under the name of Sheela-na-gig, found in medieval churches and castles. The usual characteristics of Sheela-na-gig are 'an ugly, mask-like skull-face with a huge scowling mouth, skeletal ribs, huge genitalia held apart with both hands, and bent legs', offering a fantasy of unlimited sexual licence but at the same time a comic reminder of our origins. Such figures, expressing the intimate and awesome sight of the birth mystery and symbolizing the moment when the bloody placenta is severed and new life released, indicate the depth of meaning that underlies the grotesque humour of some of the Celtic tales.

In the Irish story *The Destruction of Da Derga's Hostel*, the hostel symbolizes the royal abode of the body. After sunset, three monsters – the triple goddess in her Kali or devouring-mother aspect – arrive at one of the seven doors and demand to be admitted. On the night of the new year, Samhain (or Hallowe'en), between midnight and dawn – the time between times – they cannot be refused. The face of one hag is described as being so ugly that if 'her snout were flung up on a branch and stuck there . . . her lower lip would reach her knees'. The second has 'lips on the side of her head . . . and her lower beard hanging as far as her knees'. The triad is made up by a hideous one-eyed and one-legged black creature carrying a pig under his one arm. The ancient race of the Fomori were usually described so, and characterized the giants of night perpetually in conflict with the Celtic Tuatha Dé Danann or children of the goddess.

The ritual progression of the tale, and the gradual destruction of the hostel, also suggest that the story may be a symbolic account of a Celtic burial in which the possessions, dependents and even the family were ritually burned with the body of the dead chief.

As the giver and taker of life, the triple goddess presided over the birth, mating and death of the king, her earthly consort. (Thus the rites to the Indian goddess Durga included the sacrifice of a pig or boar, and the demon priest-king who made the sacrifice represented death. At the end of the festival the Kali image of Durga was immersed in water to hide her from the rays of the morning sun.) Ritual kingship seems to have been an occasion for human sacrifice. Robert Graves, in *The White Goddess*, summarizes this ritual, as reflected in myths from many European and Middle Eastern sources. He gives the royal victim the name of the Greek hero Hercules, whose strength and potency make him a symbol of the vitality of plant life.

At midsummer, by the end of his annual reign, Hercules is made drunk with mead and led into the middle of a circle of twelve stones arranged around an oak. The oak has been lopped into a T-shape. Hercules is bound to it with willow thongs in the five-fold manner which joins wrists, neck, and ankles together. He is then beaten, flayed, blinded or castrated, impaled upon a mistletoe stake and finally hacked into joints on the altar stone. All this is done with the utmost ceremony, and his blood, caught in a stone basin, is sprinkled over the whole tribe. All those present partake of the body of the dead king to make them vigorous and fruitful.

Hercules, recognizable by his lion-pelt and club, reappears in many guises in the art and legends of the Celtic lands. The Irish Dagdá, the Good God, with his club that can kill and restore life, his garment made from a wild beast's skin, and his huge unwieldy shape, has many affinities with the Hercules myth – as has the vast hill figure of the Cerne Abbas Giant in England. The awe and fear that such gods emanated, and psychic memories of ancient agrarian rites, heighten the comic relief in popular myth. Once known as the Lord of Perfect Knowledge, the Dagdá in one tale was ignominiously given a porridge poured into a great hole in the earth, and it included 'whole goats and sheep, halves of pork and quantities of lard' which he dug out with a ladle big enough to hold a man and a woman lying side by side. The sexual qualities of this god are always explicit, and his prowess is never in doubt. Even after his enormous meal he still managed to shaft the daughter of his enemy Tetra, 'although not without difficulty', and she in turn promised to undo her father 'by depriving him of the blood of his heart and the kidneys of his courage'.

The Dagdá's mating with the goddess Morrígan, or his straddling the river-goddess Boann for a nine-month-long night of pleasure, are crude and simple literary embellishments of a ritual marriage between two prime forms of the elemental godhead. One of the functions of popular myth and legend lies in reducing such beings from their terrifying psychic level to rude figures of fun; in Irish tales such memories are usually extrapolated into hilarious descriptions of godly attributes in terms of food and sex.

Heroic Realms

The old idea that people are the guardians of the earth, and that land belongs to the whole tribe and by proxy to the godhead, is echoed in a variety of Celtic place-names stemming from the sun god Lugh. His name may have affinities with the Latin *lux*, light, or *lucus*, grove; and Laon and Lyons in France, Leyden in Holland, and Carlisle (Caer Lugubalion) in Britain were named after him. Lugnasadh, one of the great Irish games festivals, was held in honour of the god on 1 August. Other gods such as Bél, Don and Óg also personified aspects of supernatural powers to the Celtic tribes scattered throughout the Northern European river valleys and uplands; but Lugh provides an essential link between place-names, festivals and the Irish legends and stories.

The main body of stories, and the most interesting, centre around the warrior incarnation of the Celtic gods, which reflects the dominant characteristic of this extrovert tribal group. The Irish identified themselves with their gods, as the Tuatha Dé Danann – and the greatest warrior of all was the Sun himself, the victor in the eternally renewed battle with darkness. Lugh of the Long Arm possessed a magic spear that flashed fire and roared aloud in the battle of Moytura, while liberating King Nuada and the Tuatha Dé Danann from the Fomori, the one-eyed demons of the night.

Before the battle Lugh demanded entrance to this company and claimed in turn that he was a carpenter, a smith, a champion and a harper; when he won a game of chess Nuada admitted him and entrusted him with the defence of Ireland. The preparation for this battle shows the legendary heroes with specific social attributes: Goibniu the smith can fashion any weapon; Diancecht the physician, who made a silver arm for King Nuada, can cure every wounded man; Credne the brazier makes rivets for the spears, hilts for the swords and bosses and rims for the shields; the Dagdá has his famous club, his cauldron of plenty which no one can leave without being satisfied, and his harp that can play three airs, the sleep strain, the grief strain and the laughter strain.

In the battle, Lugh knocks out the single evil eye of the king of the Fomori with a stone from a sling, and since it falls through the back of his head it consumes many of the Fomori. The rest of the pirates flee in their ships and henceforth these 'one-eyed, one-legged and one-armed' creatures are no longer a threat. The great epic *Táin Bó Cúalgne*, 'The Cattle Raid of Cooley', shows the warrior hero Cú Chulainn single-handedly defending the Northern Province against 'the Men of Ireland'. In one episode, when the champion is badly wounded and needs a respite, the sun god Lugh himself appears, walking unconcernedly through the carnage of the battle. 'Who are you?' Cú Chulainn asks the ghost warrior. 'Your father from the Outerworld am I, . . . Lugh, son of Ethliu. Sleep a while, Cú Chulainn,' says the radiant warrior, 'and I will oppose all during that time.' He examines each wound so that it becomes clean. Then he sings him the 'men's low strain' so that Cú Chulainn falls asleep.

To be a warrior among warriors was the ideal life for the Celt, but to die in a fight surrounded by friends, poets and a hundred dead enemies was the supreme consummation. Such an attitude to death and reincarnation is difficult for the modern Western mind to grasp. Essentially, the free flow of consciousness is viewed in terms of a 'realm of nothingness' whose pivot is life; and, as Buddha said of his enlightenment under the Bo tree at Benares: 'the cause of life . . . is death'.

The preparation for the supreme moment, from his initiation onwards, gave the Celtic warrior his fearlessness and pride. Such qualities were noticed and commented upon by all the classical Greek and Roman writers, who also refer to the Celts' love of fighting and easy attitude to death. In the Cú Chulainn story, the sun god materializes to take over the functions of the warrior, who by dying for three days can remain mortal. In this bardo state he can ascend the three mystical worlds of the Celtic afterlife: from earth-body to the physical spirit and finally into the radiant soul-light in which the sun himself is manifest. When Cú Chulainn sleeps he becomes joined to his own embodied radiance, inhabiting all worlds at once.

This easy movement between the human warrior hero and his otherworldly archetype, the sun god, is a common practice in every kind of Celtic story. This is the key to the Celtic Mysteries – the merging of the spiritual, physical and imaginative planes. The later Christian insistence on a duality between light and darkness, between body and soul, between this reality and the other numerous possibilities in time and space, was unknown to the Celts; and it accounts, for example, for the many confusions centring on the Arthurian legend.

Arthur may well have been a historical figure, a sixth-century British military leader; but his importance is as a mythical hero: an immortal solar warrior. He is the most popular and the most romantic of the Celtic sun heroes. Ancient myths coalesced around his name to form the 'Matter of Britain', the series of great medieval romances whose fascination shows no signs of diminishing. The commemoration of Arthur in place-names throughout Britain is a localization of a European affiliation with Lugh and other Celtic heroes. The transformation of Merlin from a seven-year-old boy wonder, who confounds the Druidic priests by obliterating a pair of water-dragons undermining the foundations of a royal fort, into the seer and mentor of the new solar archetype, is a common theme. Arthur, son of Uther Pendragon, has a close mythical association with St Michael, as the Lord of Light putting down the dragon-powers of darkness; and St Michael, in turn, who is shown holding the scales and weighing the souls on some Irish stone crosses, becomes a reincarnation of Thoth, Egyptian god of the Underworld. In Islamic tradition Michael was the angel to whom God gave the controlling force to execute his will in the universe of wind and rain. In a Celtic context, without the Christian need for a moral duality showing good and evil as separate forces,

Michael as a solar entity is the primal force that holds the angelic and earthly elements of his own nature in balance.

The Celtic Mysteries took shape in the flux of in-between states, such as the twilight between light and dark or night and day, or in the dew that was neither rain nor sea-water, nor river nor well-water; and used the sacred mistletoe that was neither a plant nor a tree. The ghost warrior from the Sidh, 'a man born not of woman', tells Cú Chulainn to sleep, 'for they have no power over your life at this time'. In the bardo state the hero is neither dead nor awake; like Arthur asleep below a hillside, he is a 'once and future king' – ritually bound as a cosmic embodiment of the Ancient dream state.

The area of expected flux, full of omens, signs and other extraordinary events, was indeterminate; and against it the warrior could pit his life. The constants of this life-style, enumerated in the teachings of the American Indian sage Don Juan, are characterized by four qualities. To be a warrior one has to have respect, to be aware of fear, to be wide-awake at all times and to be self-confident. From his initiation onwards, the warrior's own special reaction to danger could be summed up as 'an awareness of intent'.

For Cú Chulainn this 'intent' took the most extraordinary form, almost like an epileptic state, called the warp-spasm. Its phallic content is evident: 'He blew up and swelled like a bladder full of breath and bent himself in a fearful hideous arch, mottled and terrifying.' On one occasion, when the rage and fury seized him, he captured a wild stag and tied it behind his chariot, and, with a flock of captured swans ahead of him and three bloody dripping heads in one hand, charged around the royal fort in the insulting left-handed manner demanding a fight. The king sent out his wife and the other women, naked, with a vat of cold water, to calm the warrior. 'The vat burst asunder about him. They thrust him into another vat and it boiled with bubbles the size of fists. He was placed at last in a third vat and he warmed it till its heat and cold were equal. Then he got out and Queen Mugain gave him a blue cloak to go around him with a silver brooch in it, and a hooded tunic.'

Blood and feasting sustained the Celtic warrior. Cattle raiding, as with the sacred bulls of the *Táin Bó Cúalgne*, was the commonest cause of war. At feasts the warriors competed in boasting matches for the honour of carving the first portion. After many exchanges around Mac Dá Thó's pig, Cet Mac Magach sits down by it with a knife in his hand to cut the champion's portion and invites any northern warrior to challenge his right to do so. Fellow after fellow rises, only to be put down by Cet in such an insulting and devastating manner that the others are forced to retire. He taunts them with their failures and shortcomings: one has been blinded, another has lost his testicles in their last encounter, and the king's son, nicknamed the 'Stammerer of Macha', is so called because of a spear wound in the throat from Cet. As Cet is about to carve the pig, Conall the Victorious, one of the greatest Ulster heroes, enters the hall. Cet and Conall compliment each other on their valour and then Cet is told to get up from the pig. Ever since he first took up arms, Conall says, he has not let a day go by without killing a Connachtman and sleeping with his head under his knee. 'It is true, said Cet, you are the better man, but if Auluan were here he would give you contest for contest. It is a blot on us that he is not here. But he is here, said Conall, drawing Auluan's head from his belt; and he hurled it at Cet, hitting him on the chest, so that a rush of blood broke over his lips.'

Posidonius, travelling through Gaul late in the second century BC, encountered the Celtic head-hunters: 'When they depart from the battle they hang the heads of their enemies from the necks of their horses, and when they have brought them home, nail the spectacle to the entrance of their houses.' Like most anthropologists, Posidonius hated the sight at the beginning, but later, having seen it in many places, he could bear it calmly enough to write about it. Livy also described a ceremony in which the head of an enemy chieftain was placed in a temple – a reminder of their custom of decking skulls with gold and using them as drinking vessels. Diodorus and Strabo refer to the Celtic custom of embalming the heads of distinguished enemies in cedar oil, to be shown off with great pride to visitors. Collecting and comparing 'brain balls' seems to have been a favourite pastime in many of the warrior tales, especially when they fell to arguing over the champion's portion: 'When they dine, they have hearths with big fires and cauldrons, and spits loaded with big joints of meat, and some of the company often fall into an altercation and challenge one another to single combat; they make nothing of death.' For once the classical writers and the Irish poets had been to the same movie.

Shamans and Rituals

The association of the Druids with oaks, mistletoe and the annual outing at Stonehenge is probably the extent of popular knowledge of this powerful group of priests, administrators and poets. Their veneration of the 'sacred oak groves', their mistletoe rites, and their other rituals in forests or on hill-tops – 'without the use of temples' – were part of a widespread animistic belief that trees, like the large stone monoliths, were embodiments of the spirits of dead ancestors, and identified with the forces of nature. The Druids were shamans. Through a process of personal initiation, in a succession of trance states, they gained access to the Otherworld; they could represent each world within the other.

We know, from Gallo-Roman carvings, of a horned god called Cernunnos, whose origins lie in the kind of deity whom anthropologists call the 'lord of the animals'. He was the god of the chase, and the quarry was in his power. He appears in British folklore as 'Herne the Hunter', and Shakespeare mentions his oak in Windsor Forest. The idea of a horned huntsman goes back to a very ancient level; cave paintings show a man in a wild animal's skin. The hunter identified with the stag – made it, indeed, the ancestral symbol of his clan – in order to propitiate its ruling spirit. This is a very ancient mystery, although not a purely Celtic one: hunter and hunted are one.

Shape-shifting into our animal natures, whether as bull, stag, horse, boar, cat, bird or fish, is a common feature of Celtic tales. Such attempts at tapping latent powers and extending the range of consciousness through strictly observed rituals have long been recognized as the special gift of certain individuals. They enter a collective dream state where past and present, psychic and physical realities merge, to become the bridge between divine and animal aspects of man: these individuals, in all nomadic societies, are the shamans.

In their close identification with the spirits and forces of nature, the Greek writer Sotian likens the Druids to the Magi of Persia and the Brahmins of India; the originators of the study of philosophy, but uttering it in riddles. This may be a reference to their use of triads as a mnemonic device, as in this sample from the Triads of Ireland:

'What are the three dumb creatures that give knowledge to everyone? Not hard to say: an eye, a mind, a letter.' This is still a succinct and common method for exchanging information among children; and, since the Celtic poet had to know hundreds of tales, this question-and-answer method was a test that would reveal his ability, his quick wit and his manner of speech. In the Irish *Colloquy of the Two Sages*, the elder, Firchertne, asks the younger man, Néde, his name. Néde, who has put on a false beard to make himself look older and sits in the other's chair, replies *Ni ansa, robec, romor rothet rochtot* ('Not hard to say: very small, very great, very sharp, very brittle'), and follows it with a 'rhetoric' that was probably originally a Druidic naming or initiation chant:

> *Anger of fire*
> *fire of speech*
> *breath of knowledge*
> *wisdom of wealth*
> *sword of song*
> *song of bitter-edge*

At the end of a long series of such exchanges in which the sages communicate entirely, as Sotian says, 'in riddles', Firchertne is asked for 'tidings' and replies with a seven-page prophecy foretelling the tribulations that will mark the end of the world.

The form of this colloquy may be based on the oral examination in the seventh year of bardic training; but its origins go back much further. Riddles and sophisticated word-play are a reminder of the origin of all sacred mysteries: Breath, or the Word itself. Significantly, such verbal duels are common in cultures where shamanism survives; two men rouse each other to a pitch of intense excitement so that the older man can make the tribal prophecy. At the end of the colloquy Néde kneels before his elder, saying: 'Firchertne is a great poet and prophet.'

The shamanistic identity with animals was clearly reflected in Celtic ritual even in Christian times. In AD 1185, the Welsh historian Giraldus Cambrensis was horrified by what he called a 'barbarous and abominable rite of enthronement' practised by an Ulster clan, and in his *Description of Ireland* he describes it all very clearly: 'The whole people of the country being gathered in one place, a white mare is led into the midst of them, and he who is to be inaugurated, not as a prince but as a brute, not as a king but as an outlaw, comes before the people on all fours, confessing himself a beast with no less impudence than imprudence. The mare being immediately killed and cut into pieces and boiled, a bath is prepared for him from the broth. Sitting in this he eats of the flesh which is brought to him, the people standing around and partaking of it also. He is then required to drink of the broth in which he bathes, not drinking it in any vessel nor even in his hand but lapping it with his mouth. These unrighteous rites duly accomplished, his royal authority and dominion are ratified.'

In the Asuamedha, a Hindu horse-sacrifice, it is the queen who performs the rite. She submits to a simulated union with the beast that is expounded by the priest in an explicit liturgical commentary. Then the horse is dismembered and the rite continues much the same as above. In India the queen unites herself with the animal incarnation of the powers of fertility; and in Ireland it was the king who accomplished the rite with a female incarnation of the same powers. Such rituals belong to the most ancient levels of Indo-European consciousness; to the time when man and beast lived in close harmony and communication; and the great tribal assemblies were occasions when the meaningful bond between the earth and its people was fully manifested.

The Celtic warrior viewed his destiny as being preordained and 'death as the centre of a long life'. The death of a king or chief was always the occasion for the tribe to assemble for the ritual burning, remembering his brave deeds and engaging wholeheartedly in the funeral games. Caesar said of the Celts that 'their funerals are magnificent and costly, and all that they think dear to them when alive they put into the fire, even animals. And shortly before this generation, the slaves and dependents that they loved were buried along with them in the funeral rites.' Mela confirms this: 'They burn and bury along with the dead whatever is of use to them when alive, and there are sons who, of their own free will, cast themselves on the funeral pyres of their relatives, expecting to live along with them.'

The well-known Irish wakes and funeral games which ritually re-enact parts of the ancient burial practices have always been loud and humorous, with plenty of dancing, singing and elaborately mimed phallic rituals. As one wit put it: 'the life of man is bound to death by way of reproduction, and only relieved by a good story'. Our present-day casual attitude to the death ceremony is probably unique in the history of the planet, and a sad comment upon our barbaric civilization.

The inauguration and selection of the new king or chief was as complex, costly and grand as the burial of the old one. The first stringent rule in Ireland was that no one with a physical blemish could rule as king. The historic King Cormac was forced to abdicate when he lost an eye, for it was unthinkable to expect the divine incarnation to manifest as a one-eyed man. Mention is made in the eleventh-century *Book of the Dun Cow* of a ritual by which a king was selected: 'A white bull was killed and the shaman-priest ate his fill of the flesh and drank its blood. A spell was chanted over him as he lay bloated in a trance-state so that he could see in the dream sphere, the shape and appearance of the man who should be made king.'

The sophisticated and urbanized classical writers were familiar with the 'natural religion' of the barbarians; but their imagination seems to have swept them away when confronted with the great forests of Northern Europe, 'when dark night fills the sky' and 'the priest himself dreads the approach and fears to surprise the lord of the grove'. They misjudged the great love of nature that sustained the Celts in every aspect of their life. Some of the most beautiful early poetry reflects this rapport between man and his physical surroundings. Together with the rituals, legends, laws and folklore, such poetry was preserved mainly in Ireland. This example, with its running sequence of triads, dates from the ninth century AD:

> *I have news for you: the stag bells, winter snows, summer has gone,*
> *Wind high and cold, the sun low, short its course, the sea running high.*
> *Deep red the bracken, its shape is lost; the wild goose has raised its accustomed cry.*
> *Cold has seized the birds' wings; season of ice, this is my news.*

The classical writers tell us very little about the social aspect of the ritual involvement with nature. The ancient place of worship would also be used for important tribal meetings and decisions, and for games, dances and feastings. The widespread Celtic word *nemeton* contains the double function of such groves, as in Drunemeton, a place of reunion of the Galatian council in Asia Minor, Medionemeton, in Scotland, and Nemetobriga, in Spanish Galicia.

The tribal wealth, comprising large quantities of gold and silver objects under the protection of the local deity, probably accounts for the Roman desecration of Celtic sacred temples. The native shrines and sanctuaries were situated in forests, by lakesides, and later in structures such as the wooden temple at Heathrow in Middlesex or the stone one at Roquepertuse in Provence. The lake site Llyn Cerrig Bach on Anglesey contained a large number of weapons, bronzes, furniture, tools and ornaments. The shrine was probably in use up to the period when the Romans destroyed the sacred groves of the Druidic centre on the island in AD 60. The scene that confronted the Roman soldiers, described by Tacitus in terms of blood-stained groves, howling priests and black-clad, screaming women brandishing firebrands, no doubt justified the imperial policy of removing the leaders of opposition by any means.

It is clear that human sacrifice was practised among the Celts, as it had been among all ancient peoples. Julius Caesar tells of mass burnings of human and animal victims in huge wickerwork figures; his testimony is suspect, and yet the image is unforgettable. In Ireland the bloody rites of the oversized god Crom Cruach, Lord of the Mound, or Bowed One of the Mound, are mournfully echoed by an anonymous monk writing in the eleventh century *Book of Leinster*.

> *. . . They did evilly*
> *Beat on their palms, thumped their bodies,*
> *Wailing to the monster who enslaved them,*
> *Their tears falling in showers.*
> *In rank stood twelve idols of stone;*
> *The figure of Crom was in gold.*

Another source states that during the legendary reign of King Tiernmas (sixteenth century BC) 'the firstlings of every issue and chief scions of every clan were offered in sacrifice to the god Crom' on the Plain of Adoration, at Mag Slecht in County Cavan. Strabo (second century BC) says that Druid augurs read the omens by killing a human victim with a sword stroke in the back and noting the way he fell, the nature of the convulsions, and the flow of blood.

According to Justin, the Celts were more skilled at divination than other people of his time, and abided by it wholeheartedly. It was a flight of birds that guided the Gauls who invaded Illyrium. On another occasion the manner of an eagle's flight convinced a Galatian king that he should turn back from an expedition and avoid disaster. Artemidorus relates that in a certain harbour in Gaul there were two crows with their wings tinged with white. If two people were in litigation, they would put cakes on a board, each arranging his own in such a manner as to avoid confusion. The crows would swoop down, eat one lot of cakes and scatter the others. The disputant whose cakes were scattered won the case.

The *Táin Bó Cúalgne* is full of anecdotes showing that divination, prophecy and magic of all kinds were common in Ireland. The story opens on the most direct note possible. A queen is sitting on the grass. The Druid passes by, and she asks him what is the present hour good for. 'For begetting a king on a queen,' he answered. The girl saw no other male near so she took him inside her. Much of the narrative is taken up by hand-to-hand fighting, so the ancient methods of healing with magic herbs, incantations and charms are emphasized. An essential part of such homoeopathic medicine was the knowledge of how to blend the correct parts of certain roots, leaves and blossoms so that all the necessary trace elements would produce the desired result. The time of the year, and of the day or night, and certain phases of the moon that were considered lucky or unlucky, were all vital aspects of Druidic healing.

The lore of the trees, or Ogham, became part of a secret language by which different aspects, qualities and uses of trees could be repeated like nursery rhymes: 'How many groups of Ogham? Answer three, namely eight chieftain trees and eight peasant trees and eight shrub trees'. The eight noble trees – birch, alder, willow, oak, rowan, hazel, apple, ash – formed the initial consonants of an ancient cryptic alphabet, the Beth-Luis-Nion, that could be used as a seasonal calendar if necessary. There were many kinds of Ogham for different parts of the body; thus a tic-tac hand language used the joints of the fingers as letters. Such dactylological codes could be quite useful in the feasting halls and night-long banquets where honour was always seen to be done and the protocol of the spoken word had pre-eminence.

The Celts love style, and their admiration for eloquence is unbounded. The Greek writer Lucian, who was travelling around Gaul during the second century BC, described a charming symbolic scene. An old man, clad in a lion skin, with a beaming smile, led a group of followers whose ears are attached to his tongue by thin gold and amber chains. They followed him eagerly, praised him and danced around him. The explanation that Lucan was given was that the old man, named Ogmios (an echo of the Druidic Ogham), represented eloquence, for it grew with age, and was more powerful than brute strength, hence the lion-skin of Hercules.

The Druid was shaman, priest, poet, philosopher, physician, judge and prophet. His initiation included several intermediate stages. Thus, the course of study for an Irish bard or *fili* included verse forms, composition and recitation of tales, the study of grammar, Ogham, philosophy and law. The next seven years were for more specialist studies and included the secret language of the poets as the *fili* became an *ollamh*. He could then acquire the knowledge of genealogy, and the committal of events and laws into poetic forms to become a doctor of law. Finally the 'man of learning' would be fit to study incantations, divination and magical practice. 'Thus every druid a bard, though every bard did not aspire to be a druid.'

Caesar, describing the priesthood of Gaul, divides them into three groups: 'The Vates practised soothsaying and studied natural philosophy. The Bards celebrated the brave deeds of their gods in verse. The Druids were concerned with divine worship, the due performance of sacrifices, both private and public, and the interpretation of ritual questions.' Their power seemed to be absolute, for in his observations the hardest penalty that could be levied on a person or family was exclusion from the sacrifices.

Any such exclusion from Celtic society would be done with proper ceremony and dignity. An account in the *Book of Ballymote* shows the ritual sanctions available to a poet if a king refused him his proper reward for a poem. After fasting on the land of the king, a council of ninety could be called to give a judgment, and if they decided that it would be a greater crime to prevent the satire or curse on the king, the poet could continue with his ritual action. At sunrise, he and six other poets would stand on a hilltop at the boundary of seven lands. The face of each poet would face his own land, and the *ollamh* or holder of the highest degree towards the land of the king. With their backs against a hawthorn on the hilltop, and a thorn from it and a slingstone in each poet's hand, and the wind blowing from the north, each of them chanted into the stone and the thorn, the *ollamh* chanting before the others, and they afterwards all together. Each would then put his stone and thorn at the butt of the tree. If they were in the wrong the earth of the hill would swallow them up. And if their magic was powerful enough, the earth would swallow the king, his wife and his sons, his horses and his hounds, his arms and his dress.

It is tantalizing that the Druid himself, the most potent member of the hierarchy, is never mentioned, except in a derogatory way, in the written Irish texts. The opposition of the Christian missionaries to them as priests of the indigenous populations may help to explain many of the anomalies in the Irish tales. There seems to have been a deliberate suppression of all that relates to religion or the exercising of priestly functions. Of course, by the ninth century, when the Irish monks began to transcribe the oral tales, the ancient religion may have been in such disrepute that it blurred into the imaginative fantasy of the tales themselves.

Within the larger Celtic community of Western Europe (never more than a patchwork of loose confederations), the Druids were the custodians of vision and prophecy, sacrifice, poetic lore, the ritual calendar and the law – all the elements which united the different groups. The ritual traditions they maintained were oral ones, of course; and once more Ireland (a country where the written word was introduced late to a still intact Celtic society) provides the best source of information.

> *When the harvest month began*
> *After a lapse of three years span,*
> *Daily seeking victor's praise*
> *Riders racing through seven days.*
> *Settlements of tax and due,*
> *Legal cases to review,*
> *Laws to publish and declare,*
> *This the business of the fair.*

This extract from a long early poem in the *Book of Rights* gives some idea of the general assembly at Tara in Ireland. If any man committed violence during that week, he was put to death, and not even the king had power to pardon him. Apart from the games, the main business of the gathering was the laws, which, like some of the ancient Indian codes, were in verse and were enshrined in the memories of those who administered them. The chief jurist stood by the king, repeating the laws one by one before a great convention of Druids, jurists and poets. Some of the laws were altered or amended; and when the task was finished the poets once more reduced the revised laws to verse, that they might be more easily retained in memory.

The Celts used an extraordinary simple method of incorporating the monthly lunar cycle with the biological life rhythm, in that their four great festivals were held every three years, each nine months after the previous one. The thirty-six-month ritual cycle had alternating good and bad months, naturally subdividing into old and new moons. The fourfold square, with the centre as the unifying principle, seen clearly in the relationship between Tara as the sacred centre and the Four Provinces of Ireland, can be viewed like an expanding mandala, so that even the hours of the day had special significance and a place in the cosmic order. The Coligny Calendar, a fragmentary bronze tablet showing a cycle of sixty-two consecutive months marked as *mat*, auspicious, and *anm*, inauspicious, obviously reflects a much more complex system. However, its late date – the first century AD – and the attempt at grafting Roman solar and lunar thinking on to the basically simple Celtic cycle, indicate the Romanization process that eventually assimilated Celtic Gaul.

The Irish ritual calendar began with the great Samhain festival gathering on 1 November. It was a pastoral affair, a time when the harvest fruits had been gathered and offerings made to the ancestors to share in the general good fortune. This custom is still observed in Ireland, in the cleaning of the house and leaving of food for the family spirits at Hallowe'en.

Lugnasadh was the main summer festival, held on 1 August. The chariot racing and other games may have been inaugurated to celebrate the sacking of Delphi. There, the snake rites that had centred around the oracle goddess Pythia were forbidden by Apollo, the Greek Lugh, who began the outdoor games festival. In Gaul, the annual fair at Lugdunum (Lyons) was changed so that it could be reconvened under the patronage of the deified Emperor Augustus. In Ireland and parts of Scotland Lugnasadh still survives as the Lammas cattle fair, which is a reminder of how important stock-raising was to the Celts.

Beltane was celebrated on 1 May, as the great spring/summer fertility gathering symbolized by the lighting of the May fires. Livestock were driven between the twin flames, and the dancing was a ritual enactment of the sun's movement through the skies. The Maypole dance and other folk rituals have their origin in the mad dance around the May fires as the whole tribe would celebrate the resurgence of the primeval life force.

Imbolc, on 1 February, was closely associated with the sacred flame that would purify the land and encourage fertility and the emergence of the sun from its winter sleep. On that day the rites of prognostication and trial marriage would take place. Until a few years ago, young men and women would gather at Teltown in County Meath and then walk towards each other, kiss and be wed. Such weddings, which could be broken the following year by walking apart, were probably the final remnants of ancient Celtic customs in which the woman had equal rights with the man in making or breaking a marriage. The ceremony of the white stones in the fire, recorded in many parts of Ireland, is another throwback to ancient times that has lost its prime significance over the centuries. White stones, bearing the names or personal marks of all the young men, were placed in the great Imbolc fire. When it had died down and cooled enough to take out the stones, each person searched for his mark and as soon as he found it would run as fast as possible from the spot. Failure to find your stone was originally a sign that the gods of the fire had bestowed supreme honour on you by choosing your life-spirit to be sacrificed for the purification and general good of the whole tribe.

Wonder Voyages

More than any other people of Western Europe, the Celts have kept the wandering spirit alive in their culture. In epic literature the journey is symbolic of the life of the soul, the cycle of experience which it must undergo.

The reasons for the Celtic expansion, in successive waves, in the first millennium BC, are obscure; but it may have been a religious impulse, in the manner of that in which the Hopi tribes expressed their constant need of movement. Their spiralling out from the Sacred Centre over the North American continent in the four directions and back again was patterned on a universal plan of world creation and maintenance which gave meaning to their ceremonies and rituals. Each movement out from the Centre articulated a vision of life in which 'the telling of our journeys is as much a religion as the ceremonies themselves'. This view could summarize the Celtic love of wandering and storytelling, and certainly their social organization had much in common with that of the Hopi: 'A clan is comprised of several families ... the members of each family being related through matrilineal descent and taking the clan name of the mother. The name and functions of the family are of little importance, it is the clan that counts determining the standing of the individual in both religious and social organization.'

A major migration of the Celts out from southern Germany and Bohemia moved westward through Gaul and is believed to have reached Spain before 450 BC. Around this time, another group moved over the Alps, occupied the Po river valley and wandered south as far as Rome and even Sicily. In 279 BC, other tribes moved eastwards through Macedonia, invaded Greece by way of Thrace and Thessaly, and plundered the temple at Delphi. Celtic mercenaries were common in the Greek wars of the third century BC, and nearly 20,000 Celts moved into Asia Minor and settled in the area known thereafter as Galatia. Sea trading on the western coast facilitated a series of movements from Spain around Armorica (Brittany) to Ireland and Scotland. The final great movement through Northern Europe was probably that of the Belgae, who settled in Southern Britain and also in Ireland.

The idea of flux and movement was fully integrated into the social customs of the Celtic tribes. The nobility and the class of skilled craftsmen, doctors, poets, priests and legal men sent their children to the homes of distant relatives, from an early age, for their upbringing in all aspects of war-training, crafts and general social etiquette. The fosterage was reciprocal over a large geographical area, so that in effect the children were raised without a close blood tie. In the Celtic world every aspect of social and religious behaviour was laid out in the laws, and payments for most transactions were exact, such as three *séts* for having the son of a freeman in fosterage, or thirty *séts* (fifteen spotted cows) for the son of a king. This distribution of wealth throughout a wide clan network created extraordinary stability for a millennium. It was said that at some periods there was so much commerce and travel in the Celtic realms that the Irish Sea was like an inland lake.

The early classical writers commonly referred to the Hyperborean regions, beyond the Celtic lands, as a paradise, and to the people who lived there as the happiest race, for 'they live without quarrelling and without sickness for as long as they like'. There are numerous Celtic legends surrounding the mysterious Isles of the Blest and the magnificent lands that have sunk beneath sea, such as Lyonesse, between Britain and France, or Hi Brazil, off the southwest coast of Ireland. The sea voyages in early Irish literature are examples of this ever-popular genre. In the adventures of Bran, Mael Dúin and Brendan the Christian monk, the mysterious islands they encounter are still centres in the midst of a vast sea of flux and constant change. The journey itself holds no real dangers; sea-faring people accept the sea as the major element in their lives and do not need to romanticize imaginary dangers. Much like the relationship between dreaming and sleeping, the voyage is a necessary transition in discovering the 'other' lands. The further analogy with life, death and dying is unmistakable; yet the tales themselves are concerned with 'place'. However weird the island image – such as a single giant foot sticking out from the sea with an island on top and a door at its base, or a vast, four-sided silver pillar with a gold mesh hanging from the top to the sea below, or an island with a huge beast whirling around its outer wall and turning itself inside its skin – it is a single tangible point, a dream image, memorable and all-embracing in its 'logic'. In this world, everything is as 'given' – food, love, hospitality, fear, directions or whatever is necessary for the journey – but 'taking' involves a choice that might result in instant obliteration.

After Mael Dúin and his friends have eaten in an empty island palace, one of them removes a necklace from the wall. The cat that has been playfully leaping from pillar to pillar suddenly becomes the avenging guardian of the island. He leaps through the man 'like a fiery arrow and burned him till he was but ashes'. Mael Dúin replaces the jewellery in its proper place on the wall, and they return to the sea.

The area where different worlds meet, such as the act of dying, the mist between sea and air, the twilight, the dawn, the shore at the river-ford, was of special significance for the Celts. The attempt to visualize this nebulous realm and make it tangible resulted in images such as the sea of glass, or the crystal boat that whisked many a hero off to the 'land of Promise'. In the voyage of Bran, the sea-god Manannán Mac Lir, lord of illusion, turns the sea into a flowering plain, the waves into shrubs, the fish into frisking lambs, and so the boat seems to be floating over an orchard of fruit trees. Bran has been lured away by a beautiful girl who sings him a haunting song that ends on the note:

Do not fall on a bed of sloth,
Let not intoxication overcome you,
Begin a voyage across the sea.

He and his companions reach an island where everyone either laughs with joy or stares in sadness, a fate that befalls one of the group. They eventually reach the island that was promised them. There is food and a woman waiting for every man of the company. After what seems like a year of such entertainment, Bran is persuaded to leave and the queen warns him not to touch land or he will regret it. When they return no one knows them, but the people who live in his old home say that the Voyage of Bran was one of their ancient stories. The man who was homesick jumps ashore and crumbles into dust. Bran relates his adventures, writes the story in Ogham and puts to sea again.

Mael Dúin's voyage to thirty-one extraordinary islands is unsurpassed in early voyage literature. He and companions encounter giant insects, big horses that eat each other, composite beasts and vast horse-like creatures that gallop over land and sea, weeping people, a black and white island with a brass wall dividing it and another with revolving ramparts of fire, through which beautiful people can be seen moving to the most haunting and delicate music. Some scholars have compared the succession of symbols in the Tibetan Book of the Dead, such as the four elements, colours, orders, etc., with the elemental nature of these islands as metaphysical entities: whiteness, blackness, fire, water, joy, sorrow, femininity, masculinity, youth, death and so on. The symbolism of the voyage, which has become obscured by the descriptive magic of such tales, suggests that these are the collected remains of an ancient oral tradition that charted the mysterious worlds beyond death.

'A question to you, said Columcille, to his strange visitor from another realm. What used this loch we are looking at to be in the old time? I know that, said the young man. It was yellow. It was blossoming. It was green. It was hilly. It was a place of drinking.

It had silver in it and chariots. I went through it when I was a deer. When I was a salmon. When I was a wild dog. When I was a man I bathed in it. I carried a yellow sail and a green sail. . . . I know not father nor mother. I speak with the living and the dead.'

The constant reiteration of the cycles of rebirth, and the easy movement between this physical world and the many Otherworlds in the Celtic stories, indicate the depth of their ontological preoccupation. Even the traditional warm-up of the present-day Irish storyteller has its origins in Druidic metaphysics: 'Fadófadó or a long long time ago, if I were there then, I wouldn't be there now; if I were there now and at that time, I would have a new story or an old story, or I might have no story at all.'

The visit to the 'Land of Promise' or 'the Many-coloured Land' or the 'Land of the Young' is a theme that has undergone as many variations in literature as in the ancient legends. The Latin *Navigatio Brendani*, which created the idea that St Brendan of Clonfert discovered the Americas, was very popular during the medieval period and may have actually encouraged the real explorations that occurred later. The twelfth-century *Vision of Mac Con Glinne* was a brilliant parody that summed up and used nearly all the thematic elements from the earlier tales. As is usual, the vision is only a small part of the whole story. The phantom from the Otherworld tells Mac Con Glinne that he is 'Wheatlet, son of Milklet/son of Juicy Bacon/Is mine own name/ Honeyed Butter-roll/Is the man's name that bears my bag.' The last reference is to the bag of sea-god Manannán, which holds all the treasures of the world. He then goes on a marvellous voyage in a boat of fat on a lake of milk and reaches the island which 'had earthworks of thick custard beyond the lake. Its bridge was of butter, its wall of wheat, the palisade was of bacon'. And the inside had 'smooth pillars of old cheese, beams of juicy bacon in due order, fine rafters of thick cream with laths of curds'. The sage gives him a cure-all for everything but the disease of wandering gentlemen and sages, commonly called loose bowels. After reciting the vision, Mac Con Glinne escapes with his life, cures the King of Cork of gluttony, and traps the demon in a cooking pot; the tale ends on an account of the reward due to whoever shall recite it.

Christian Heroes

> *Who is your God? And where is he?*
> *Is it in the skies he is, or in the earth,*
> *or under the earth, or upon the earth,*
> *or in the seas, or in the streams?*
> *Is he young? Is he beautiful?*
> *Has he sons and daughters?*
> *Is he one of the everliving ones?*

'And Patrick took them in hand to answer their questions and to teach them the true faith; and he told them that it was fitting they should join with the King of Glory, being as they were daughters of an earthly king.' This little story from Lady Gregory's *Book of Saints and Wonders* shows up the common themes of transition between old and new mysteries, with the wedding and death of the goddess, the divine twins and the new warrior hero. Ethne the Beautiful and Fedelm the Rosy-Red, daughters of the King of the West, had come to wash in the sacred well, which was their daily ritual. They found Patrick already there. He and his company of twelve in white robes (the traditional priesthood), with their books before them (the new knowledge), were now the guardians of the ancient sacred place. The goddesses of Ireland, 'sleeping in death', were invoked and then wedded to 'Christ, his son our husband'. On the simplistic popular level Christ, the newest heroic embodiment of the warrior god, was a reincarnation of Cú Chulainn, in so far as his death drama was predestined or determined by his life story in this earthly realm. The Christian missionaries exploited this appeal to the Celtic imagination in laying the foundations of the new religion.

The alteration in the ritual ceremonies was conducted with great courtesy on both sides during the centuries of isolation from the changes and collapse of the Roman Empire. There are some recorded exceptions, but the transition was peaceful, as the old Celtic heroes and goddesses became Christianized. St Brigid, a fifth-century holy lady who is said to have been born at sunrise on the first of February (the festival of Imbolc), and whose mother 'was in the service of a Druid', has all the characteristics of the earlier triple Goddess. The new Brigid became the patron saint of the hearth, the home, wells and healing. Her monastery was built around the sacred fire in Kildare, and the perpetual flame was kept burning until the time of the Norman invasion in the twelfth century. The sanctuary had probably once been oracular, like that of Delphi with its sacred flame, healing waters and indwelling goddess. The hymn to the new saint could as easily be sung to the ancient goddess: 'Brigid, excellent woman, sudden flame, may the bright fiery sun bring us to the lasting kingdom.'

Taking over and utilizing existing sanctuaries and temples was an officially approved policy of establishing the new religion. Gregory the Great, in AD 601, spelt it out in a letter to the missionaries of the west: 'If these temples in Britain are well built, it is requisite that they be converted from the worship of devils to the service of the true God: that the nation, seeing their temples are not destroyed, may remove error from their hearts and knowing and adoring the true God may the more freely resort to places to which they have been accustomed.'

The most popular Christian hero to emerge during this period was Columba, or Columcille, who was described by Fintan of Cloneenagh as one 'not to be compared with philosophers and learned men but with Patriarchs, Prophets and Apostles'. He had built his first monastery, with the nave pointing west rather than to the Christian east as was customary, in a clearing of a sacred grove on Derry Peninsula in the north of Ireland. He refused to cut down any of the ancient oak trees:

> I love my beautiful Derry,
> My Derry,
> My fair oak trees,
> My dear little cell and dwelling;
> O God in the heavens above
> Let him who profanes it be cursed.

There are so many references to Druidic practices and rituals in the popular stories of Columcille that it is impossible not to view him as a teacher and leader steeped in the ancient tradition. His close family ties with the kingship of Ireland, and his own extraordinary ability in creating a monastic system closely based on traditional Druidic mysteries, elevate him to the level of the ancient heroes. His attempts to reform the official Christian religion brought him into such conflict that he was excommunicated and banished from Ireland. Columcille and a number of companions then moved over to Iona off the west coast of Scotland, and he lived there for the remaining thirty years of his life. As we have seen in the warrior tales, ridicule and contempt by one's peers was worse than death, and impossible to combat.

Iona is known in Gaelic as Hi, Y or I, and has also been called Isle of Dreams or Isle of Druids. It is made up of the oldest exposed rock strata of the earth, and it is obviously one of the ancient sacred centres. The name has been likened to the temple *Ei* of the Greek Apollo, *An* or the Self-Existing-One of the Egyptians and *Yah*, the 'I am that I am' of the Hebrews. The sacred cranes of Apollo, the heralds of spring, were certainly special to Columcille. He had a young monk stand on the shore waiting for the first exhausted bird to arrive, and he promised dire penalties if the youth did not take special care before sending it off. The story of the saint copying out a famous manuscript, while the crane pecked out the eye of the king's son who was peeping through a hole in the door at the light inside, is a curious intermingling with the crane legend of Thoth or Hermes, or with that of Manannán Mac Lir, whose bag, in which he carries the treasures of the world, is made from the skin of a crane. Three of these sacred birds guarded Manannán's home, the Isle of Man, croaking out to passing travellers: 'Do not enter / Keep away / Pass by.' The accounts of Columcille's encounters with the Pictish Druids and the monster of the loch, of bringing young men back to life, and other associations with Mercury as healer, are unsatisfying and inconclusive in many ways.

The only occasion when Columcille is said to have returned to Ireland was for the Synod of Drumceatt, held in AD 574, to defend the bards who were about to be expelled as trouble-makers. He spoke on behalf of twelve hundred of them, which suggests that he was the chief Druid, and argued that their expulsion would deprive Ireland of a wealth of folklore and antiquity that could never be replaced. He suggested that they be given a small plot of land to support themselves. The eulogy that the bards sang to him as they marched around the hall was obviously not without a touch of historic irony, for in all probability it was at this convention that the Druids were stripped of their special privileges as administrators of the people and as priests of the old religion.

The new Christian communities of Iona, and other islands and isolated places around Ireland and Scotland, devoted their lives and energies to the 'three labours of the day – prayer, work, reading'. Their simple, ascetic lifestyle touched an old Celtic chord. The ecclesiastical decadence of the insular Celtic church was swept away in the new fervour that unified and redirected the Celtic warrior mystique. To the young men and women of the time, Latin was a new language, and like the use of the older technologies of stone and iron, became the means and impetus for yet another movement across Europe. Christ as the warrior archetype gave the Hibernian Mysteries a new strength. Like the heroes of old, his spirit was indomitable, his life predestined as a series of heroic deeds, and the task of bringing light into heathen Europe had a reality and function that recalled the ancient visions and heroic quests of the Celtic world.

The scattered remnants of the Celts in Brittany, Ireland, Wales and Scotland are trying to preserve what remains of their ancient European culture. It is ironic and tragic that the heritage of the sacred place which has been preserved for many thousands of years is at present in danger of being lost. It is too easy to ignore the parable of Ogmios and the skin of Hercules, or to forget what was said of Columcille, that he brought the gift of silence to the people.

The borders of our minds are ever shifting
And many minds can flow into one another . . .
And create or reveal a single mind, a single energy.

1 The Irish poet W. B. Yeats maintained that this single energy, and the great memory of nature herself, could be evoked by symbols. The greatest symbols of the ancient sacred tradition of magic and religion in western Europe are the mysterious megalithic monuments such as Stonehenge. They were built as solar and lunar observatories; foreknowledge of the solstices and equinoxes, and of eclipses, was essential for the proper functioning of the ancient social order that centred people in relation to cosmic rhythms and tribal tradition. In the earliest recorded explanation of this great solar power-house (by Geoffrey of Monmouth), Merlin was said to have moved the great bluestones from Ireland, where they had been brought from Africa by 'giants who were magicians'. Certainly every explanation begs more questions; Stonehenge, like the Great Pyramid, will remain enigmatic until the race learns to live in harmony with the spirit of the world. (Stonehenge, Wiltshire, England, seen through a fish-eye lens.)

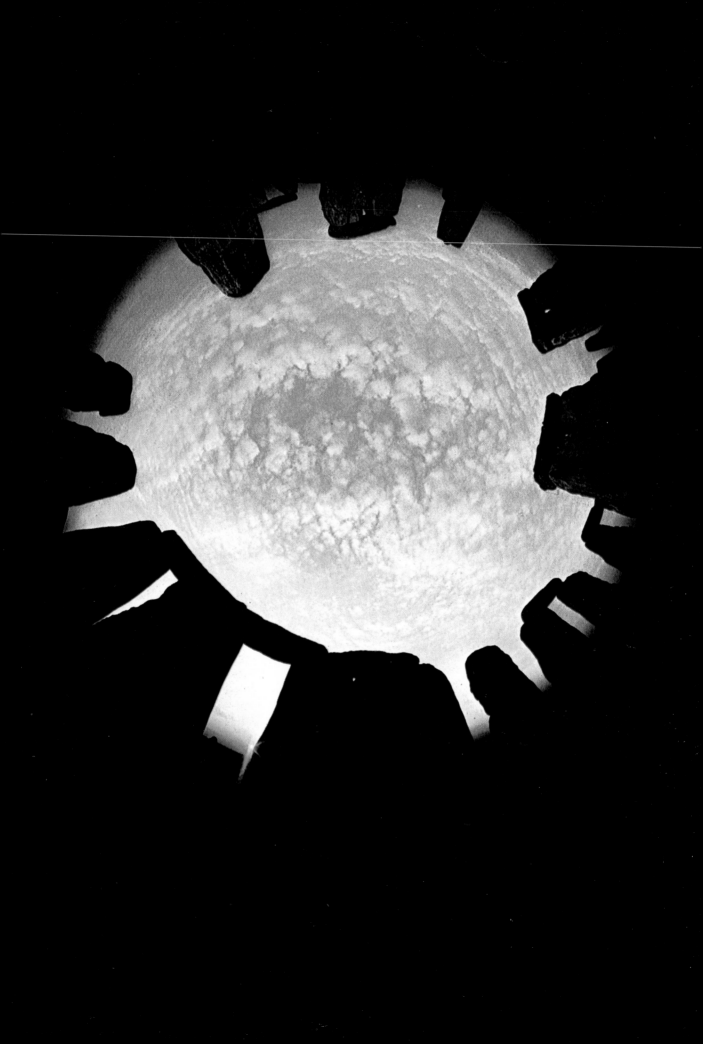

2, 3 High up on the fells, the pre-Celtic stone circle at Castlerigg (left) is a hundred feet in diameter and contains thirty-nine stones. Like certain trees, such stones were considered by the Celts to have special energy properties or to contain the spirit body of a deity or hero. The crude sandstone head (above), with its curved horns for ears, indicates that in Roman Britain there was a cult of one of the many horned gods of Celtic mythology. Their names, except that of Cernunnos (pl. 24), are now forgotten. (2 Stone circle, Castlerigg, near Keswick, Cumbria, England; 3 Stone head from Netherby, Cumbria, England, 2nd–3rd c. AD.)

4, 5 The human head was considered by the Celts to be a supreme source of spiritual power. The three-coloured design enamelled in a fourfold and eightfold square (right) is symbolically unified in the mystic Centre. The addition of one makes the sacred numbers three, five, seven and nine. The triple goddess appears as both one and three forms; the Four Provinces of Ireland, grouped about the Centre, were always referred to as Fifths; and the seven oars on each side of the tiny gold boat (below) represent the seven openings of the body. The sea god Manannán Mac Lir, with his magical powers of creating illusion, carried the Celtic heroes to the Otherworld beneath the sea. Such themes, often obscured in the necessity of a good story, recur endlessly in Celtic ritual and legend. (4 Gold boat from Broighter, Co. Derry, Ireland, 1st c. AD; 5 Handle of Irish bowl from a ship burial at Miklebostad, Norway, 9th c. AD.)

6 The type of grotesque effigy known as the Sheela-na-gig is a graphic representation of the Celtic goddess of creation and destruction. Common in Irish castles and churches (although this example is British), its blatant sexual nature relates to male fear-fantasies of the devouring mother. This repellent Kali-aspect of the goddess recurs throughout Indo-European myth and ritual. (Corbel, church of St Mary and St David, Kilpeck, Herefordshire, England.)

7 Phallic symbolism is represented all over the Celtic realm in the prehistoric stones, whose ancient names were often elaborated with the same grotesque and savage humour that finds expression in the Sheela-na-gig. Thus, in the *Táin Bó Cúalgne*, Cú Chulainn foils King Ailill by ramming his two emissaries, his daughter and his fool, on to two standing stones called thereafter Findhabhair's Stone and the Fool's Stone. (Stone near Minions, Cornwall, England.)

8, 9 The name of these shapely hills is Dá Chích Anann, the Paps of Anu. This goddess was possibly identical with Danu, ancestral mother of the Irish Celts (who called themselves Danu's Children, the Tuatha Dé Danann), and also with Ave or Avu, the moon-queen who presided over the twin henges of the necropolis at Avebury in Wiltshire. The Cerne Abbas Giant, over 180 feet long, is cut into a chalk hillside; his knotted club and erect phallus are attributes of the fertility god Hercules. It has been suggested that a mound beneath the giant's left hand is the site of a phallic stone smashed by St Augustine when he first took over the sacred well and founded an abbey to convert the stubborn pagans of Cerne. The agrarian rites associated with phallic worship long survived as strong local folk traditions: the rectangular enclosure known as the Frying-pan or Ring, about 70 feet from the giant, was the site of the Maypole with its annual games and revels; the giant was cleaned every seven years on May Eve; and couples slept within the giant as a cure for barrenness. (8 The Paps, Co. Kerry, Ireland; 9 Hill figure, Cerne Abbas, Dorset, England, perhaps *c.* 1st c. BC.)

10, 11, 12 Nearly two hundred pieces of wood carving, including many complete figurines, were excavated in 1964 from a pool in the sanctuary of Sequana, near the source of the Seine. Although deposited there in the first century AD, they are believed to come from an earlier sanctuary on the same site. Wooden figures such as these – which may represent either a deity or the worshipper who offered them – were perhaps the commonest form of votive offering; very similar ones have been found elsewhere in the Celtic lands. It is possible that the material was as important as the form. Certainly the craftsmen who sought, either in wood or stone, to create a divine image, made only minimal changes to the natural shaping properties of their material. (10 Head of a wooden phallic figure from Ralagan, Co. Cavan, Ireland; 11, 12 Wooden votive figures from the sanctuary of Sequana, near Saint-Seine-l'Abbaye, Côte-d'Or, France.)

Overleaf

13 There is no archaeological evidence that Stonehenge was a centre for Celtic worship, but there is equally no denying its powerful psychic attraction, or the Celts' fascination with the megalithic monuments. The May ceremonies of the Celts of Britain are here imaginatively reconstructed, using imagery drawn from a common European fund of cult lore. The stones in the centre are draped with veils showing the serpent power of the Caduceus, Mercury's staff. The procession into the temple is led by the divining bard with his magic wand, followed by lesser bards with their harps. The shrine of Ceridwen, stored with corn and representing the fruitfulness of the earth, is followed by that of Helio-Arkite, the so-called Diluvian God to whom the earth was restored after the Flood. Any such reconstruction can serve only to indicate the depth of meaning that the last tribal society in Europe attached to the seasonal cycles of change. (The Festival of the Britons at Stonehenge, from Meyrick and Smith, *Costume of the Original Inhabitants of the British Islands*, London, 1815.)

C.H.S. del.

Grand Conventional

Aquatinted by R. Havell.

Festival of the Britons.

14 All sacred wells, from local springs to great healing centres such as Aquae Sulis (now Bath, in western Britain), were under the protection of the threefold mother goddess. The central figure of the divine triad as shown here has the fierce protective scowl and the running swastika posture of the Gorgon; her companions are surrounded by symbols of plenty. The well which they guarded contained numerous coin offerings, a relief showing the goddess Coventina, tiny bronze heads, animal bones and a human skull. (Relief from Coventina's Well, High Rochester, Northumberland, England, 2nd–3rd century AD; see p. 82.)

15 The Monster of Noves, with a half-eaten limb protruding from its mouth, scales on its back and huge claws clamped on twin severed heads, is a powerful emblem of fear. It clearly symbolizes the death-dealing aspect of the godhead; but its erect phallus is a reminder of the close esoteric connection between killing and fertility, death and rebirth. It corresponds to the belief that human sacrifice is necessary to promote fertility; and perhaps it was an image such as this that represented Crom Cruach, the Bowed One of the Mound, in the bloody rites of ancient Ireland. (Stone figure from Noves, Bouches-du-Rhône, France, *c.* 3rd c. BC.)

16 The great pre-Celtic Cornish burial chambers consist of a number of vertical granite slabs surmounted by a quoit or giant capstone, and originally covered with a mound of earth and stone: a symbol of the mystery of death and rebirth, and a dream place of past and present where psychic and physical realities merge. Through a process of initiation, in a succession of trance states for three days and nights inside the dark interior, the shaman priest gained access to the ancestral spirit world. The function of the man of power was to commune and identify with the forces of nature on behalf of the community. (Lanyon Quoit, Penwith, Cornwall, England, 2nd millennium BC.)

17 Julius Caesar says that the Druids, the senior of the three grades of Celtic holy men, were responsible for public sacrifice; and although his accounts of human victims burnt in wicker-work colossi are suspect (the Druids were implacable in their opposition to his conquests), it seems clear that the Celts, like other ancient peoples, did propitiate their gods by human sacrifice. (Still from the film *The Wicker Man*, written by Anthony Schaffer, directed by Robin Hardy, 1973.)

18 The neck of this 'Janus' sculpture is gripped in the bill of a goose. The bird once formed part of a pillar in a Gallic sanctuary which had a portico carved with geese and horses' heads. Both creatures were sacred, among Gauls and Romans alike, to the god of war. The reciprocal relationship between the human

hero and his divine archetype is manifest in the warrior's predestined fate, facing both life and death. The preparation for the supreme moment, from his initiation onwards, gave the Celtic warrior his zest, fearlessness and pride. (Janus head from Roquepertuse, Bouches-du-Rhône, France, 3rd–2nd c. BC.)

19 This Gallic image of a warrior's head bears a curious hood which has been variously interpreted as a stylized helmet and as part of a funerary niche. The scratched decorations in front appear to be a torc and a triad of running horses. It is possible that the hood reflects a Celtic ritual, known to us otherwise only in the mysterious figures of the Genii Cucullati of northern Britain, in which the human head is shrouded in the womb or caul of rebirth. (Warrior's head from Sainte-Anastasie, Gard, France, 1st millennium BC; see p. 82.)

20 Among the standing stones at Carnac it is easy to believe that this is the place where, according to Celtic mythology, the heroes rest on their journey to the Isles of the Blest. It is probable that, before the stones were re-set in modern times into their present three alignments, they were arranged as a star-chart. The link between Carnac and Glastonbury is obvious in the dedication of both to St Michael the dragon-slayer; one has a church on a tumulus and the other on its famous Tor. If the ten-mile landscaped zodiac around Glastonbury had a counterpart at Carnac, then these stones may well have served for the ritual re-enactment of a cosmic drama. (Morning mist at Carnac, Morbihan, France; see p. 74.)

21 Holed stones are widely believed to possess healing power. Until recent times children were passed through the Crick stone (below) to cure them of rickets. Such beliefs probably stem from the position of such stones at the entrance to prehistoric burial chambers: a symbol of the birth passage in the ancient rites of initiation and rebirth. (The Men-an-tol or Crick stone, near Morvah, Cornwall, England, *c*. 16th c. BC.)

22 The perception of the Celtic mysteries took shape in the flux of a facing-both-ways state: in twilight, in the dew, with the sacred mistletoe (see p. 11). The duality of I and Thou, or One and Another, resolves itself within the visible world of nature and the invisible realm of the dream. Here the Celtic Janus lives on, in a stone figure which sits back-to-back with its double in a remote Irish Christian graveyard. (Stone figures on Boa Island, Lough Erne, Co. Fermanagh, Ireland, *c*. 7th c. AD.)

23 The ancient Indo-European idea of the sun as a celestial warrior-king drawn through the sky on a war chariot stems from the recognition of the cyclic evolution of the powers moving earth and sky, and from the dependence of nomadic cultures on the horse in peace and war. The funeral of the hero in epic poetry, in which his body is burnt together with his horse and all his most precious worldly possessions, is the extreme expression of this dual relationship. (Votive sun chariot from Trundholm, Denmark.)

24, 25 (right) On a panel from a silver-gilt Celtic cauldron, the horned god Cernunnos demonstrates his mastery over his cult beasts, the stags. In one Irish kingship legend, five brothers (representing the Five Provinces) are lost in the snows of night. After they have killed and eaten a fawn they take shelter in the house of a hag. She invites each to lie with her; when the fifth accepts, and she turns into the most beautiful woman in the land, he knows he is the new king. On the circular base of the same cauldron a warrior god or priest sacrifices a giant bull. In the ancient stag, bull or horse sacrifices, the king united himself with the animal incarnation of divine power, before the feast when all the tribe absorbed its strength and wisdom. Tapping such powers, and extending the range of consciousness through strictly observed rituals, created a bridge between the divine and animal aspects of man. (Panels of the cauldron from Gundestrup, Denmark, 2nd–1st c. BC.)

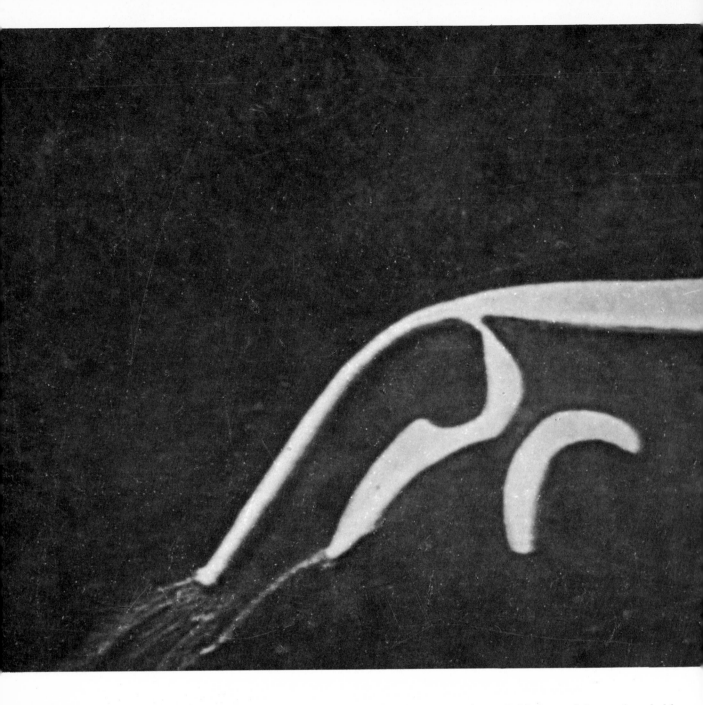

26 The Uffington White Horse marks the place as sacred to a Celtic horse deity, and probably as the site of regular ceremonial games and tribal gatherings. Its stylized design and huge scale (365 feet from nose to tail) show the devotion and artistic sophistication of its creators, probably the Belgae who moved into southern Britain and Ireland from the Continent around 300 BC. A mound below and to the left of the horse is known as Dragon's Hill. The name implies association with those occult forces within the earth which geomancers and water diviners detect. Guy Underwood's researches suggest that several images of such powers are superimposed beneath the present horse. (Hill figure of a white horse, Uffington, Oxfordshire, England, *c.* 1st c. AD.)

27 The designs on many ancient Celtic coins show a marked resemblance to the Uffington horse. It was common to have the king's head and name on the obverse and a splayed horse or horse and chariot on the reverse. The fragmentation of the figures to suggest motion may have had a special symbolism for the users of the coins. (Gold coin of the Aulerii, Britain, 1st c. BC.)

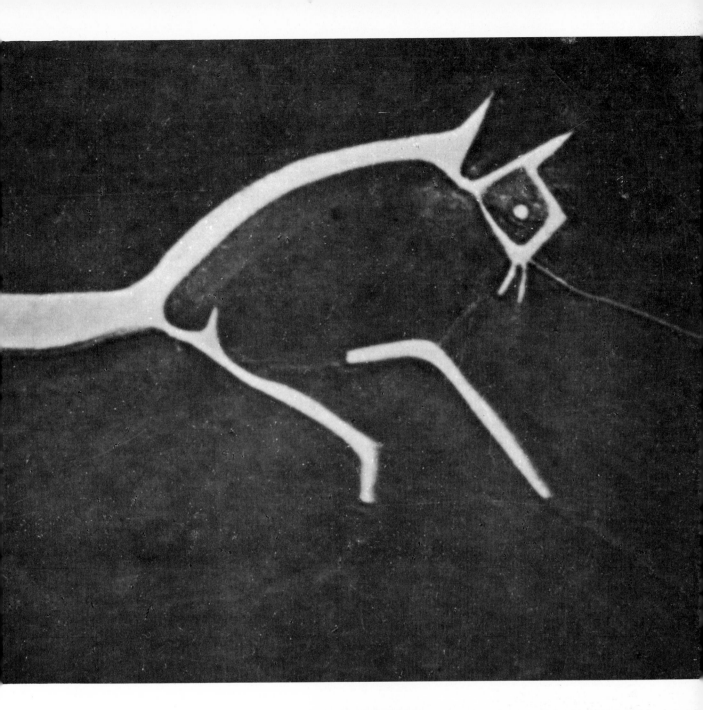

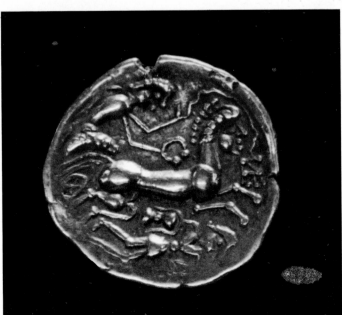

28 Celtic art and Celtic tales reflect a constant fascination with the human head. The warrior who carried off the head of a defeated enemy had more than the simple proof of his victory: he was causing the power of the sacred, which dwelt within the other warrior, to work for him. The skulls in the doorposts of this Gallic temple – the everlasting spiritual guardians of the war god – were both a concentration of power and a protection against supernatural danger. (Stone doorpost with head trophies, from Roquepertuse, Bouches-du-Rhône, France, 3rd–2nd c. BC; see p. 87.)

29 The Picts of northern Britain shared with the other Celtic tribes both their cult of the head and their special regard for the colour blue, sacred to the earth goddess. The scribes deprecated the Picts' fondness for body-painting, cannibalism and public sex; but the naked shock troops of all the Celtic nations, well attested by classical sources, must have been no less daunting to meet in battle than this vividly imagined Pict. (Pictish warrior, watercolour by John White, c. 1590.)

30, 31 The particular functioning of priests, warriors, artisans and other groups in terms of strict social codes added coherence to the many factors that made the Celtic migrations possible, such as the availability of a new iron technology, domestic animals and an expanding population. The Celts changed the conventional methods of warfare of the first millennium BC with their large iron hacking swords, their spear-throwing from fast two-horsed chariots, and their use of screaming naked riders to create initial terror and confusion. Their skill in making a wide variety of iron-based implements enabled them to open up vast tracts of land, throughout northern Europe, for the cattle grazing that became the cornerstone of their economy. Their great hilltop forts at strategic points enabled the allied Celtic tribes to control the trade routes between the west, the Mediterranean and the Middle East for almost a millennium. (30 Bronze figurine of a Celtic spearman, from the Rome area, Italy, 3rd c. BC; 31 Bronze sword-hilt decorated with head trophy, from North Grimston, Yorkshire, England, 2nd c. BC.)

32 By the sixth century AD, Christian monasticism had become an established part of Celtic social life, and many pursued a humble life of hard work and prayer in remote and inaccessible places such as Iona, Innisboffin and the Skelligs. The sanctuary here comprised two small oratories, six stone beehive huts, a small church, and a monks' garden in the form of a series of terraces that fell sharply to the shore. Between the sky and the sound of the sea, the manuscripts such as the Book of Kells – begun on Iona – became 'a mirror of God's handiwork'. (Little Skellig seen from Skellig Michael, Co. Kerry, Ireland.)

33 The Christianized Celts still lived in close psychic contact with an Otherworld that remained real to them; their culture, their art and their life continued in the unbroken rhythms of the past. Were it not that one of these stone figures holds a crozier and a bell, they could be taken for the gods of some mysterious cult site. (Saints, 9th–10th c. AD, built into wall of church, White Island, Co. Fermanagh, Ireland, 12th c.)

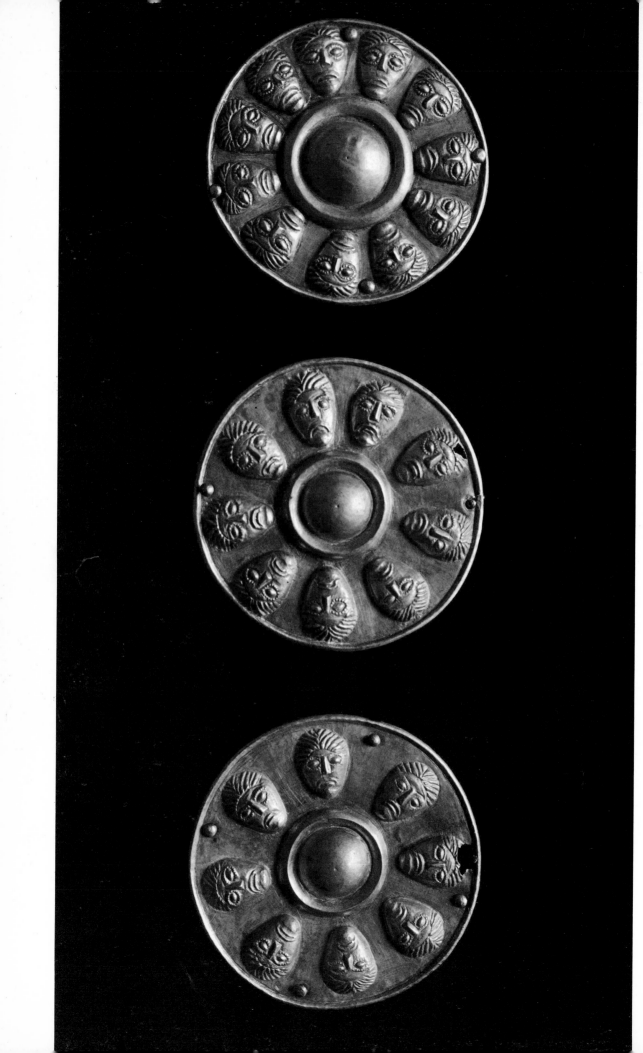

34, 35 The refinement of Celtic metalwork spans the whole period from La Tène to the Middle Ages. On these repoussé silver horse ornaments (left), tiny head trophies – protective charms like the horse brasses of more recent tradition – cluster round a central solar boss in groups of eight, nine and eleven. The roundel on the bowl of the Ardagh Chalice (right) is formed by silver ribs set with delicate gold filigree spirals and radiating in the form of a Greek cross from the central stud of blue and red glass: four quarters plus the Sacred Centre, as in the fivefold division of Ireland itself. The chalice itself, assembled from hundreds of delicately worked parts, is one of the few remaining treasures of early Christian Celtic metalwork. (34 Horse trappings from Manerbia sul Mella, Italy, 1st millennium BC; 35 Detail of chalice from Ardagh, Ireland, 8th c. AD.)

36, 37 The cult of the bell goes back to the beginnings of Celtic Christianity although no early
examples now exist. The little bronze casket made for St Patrick's bell (above), with its silver plating
and filigree, exemplifies the Celtic ornamental tradition. The three large glass gems (one now
missing), and the thirty panels plus one, show how the ancient esoteric thinking had blended with
the new religion. On the top, the cast silver openwork forms two birds whose wings, necks and
beaks spiral, enmesh and fuse into one snake-like creature on the other side. The oak and bronze
cross (right), with its central rock-crystal reliquary, was made for Turlough O Conna, High King of
Ireland, to enshrine a relic of the True Cross. The ninefold ornaments about a Sacred Centre are
unmistakably Celtic. (36 Shrine of St Patrick's Bell, Ireland, c. 1100; 37 Cross of Cong, made by
Maelisu, from Co. Mayo, Ireland, 1123–36.)

38, 39 A single monolith fur-
nishes shaft, ring and arms of the
best preserved of the Irish crosses
(left), with its separate little house
resting on top. With some minor
exceptions, the purely decorative
elements are confined to the sides
of the shaft and the base. The
extremely detailed carved panels,
showing biblical scenes such as
the arrest and Crucifixion of
Christ, indicate that the artist was
attempting an extended narrative; this was something quite
new to Celtic art, which had
always been essentially ornamental and symbolic. The old
tradition takes its revenge in the
figures of the two cats at the base
of the cross, one licking a kitten
and the other holding a mouse.
The traditions are blended more
harmoniously in the crude stone
cross on the right, on which an
Irish saint carries his invariable
attributes of bell and crozier. The
staff of life, with its great spiral
centring on the heart chakra,
shows that the artist was deep in
the ancient traditions as well as
the new. (38 Muireadach's Cross
at Monasterboice, Co. Louth,
Ireland, c. 10th c. AD; 39 Detail
of the Doorty Cross at Kilfenora,
Co. Clare, Ireland, 12th c. AD.)

40, 41 Over the centuries Celtic art continued to evoke a dense, ever-changing world in which nothing is as it first appears: a poetic and artistic realm of consciousness. As matter can fuse and become form, so a plant becomes a tail, interweaves and develops a head, legs or feet, giving rise to extraordinary pliable animals that devour each other. The artist who created the scene above, with the Angel representing the Evangelist St Matthew overlooking its endless intertwining of plant growth, shows the omnipresence of spirit in matter. On a different level, Richard Dadd drew on an ancient and essentially Celtic tradition when he showed the animate principles in nature as the 'little people' – the gods of the distant past, living on in the secret places of the imagination. Here, in a timeless moment, each being stands apart and waits on the 'master-stroke'. (40 Detail of canon-table, Book of Kells, Ireland, 8th c. AD; 41 The Fairy Feller's Master-stroke, painting by Richard Dadd, England, 1855–64.)

42, 43 Many artistic traditions, pagan as well as Christian, stand in a direct relationship
with the Celtic school of ornament which culminated in the great Irish illuminated manuscripts. A magnificent sacred bull from Scotland (above), drawn with great economy in
the true curling Pictish style, shows a use of line that can be recognized in Irish and even
Saxon art (pl. 44). A curious story is told of the Book of Durrow (right): after the
dissolution of the monasteries it was in the possession of a farmer who used to dip it in the
drinking-water to protect his cattle from disease. (42 Bull incised on a stone slab, from
Burghead, Morayshire, Scotland, 7th–8th c. AD; 43 Lion of St Mark, page from the Book
of Durrow, Irish, from Northumberland, 7th c. AD.)

44 The Saxon invasions did not destroy the Celtic traditions, even in England. This beautiful Saxon brooch, of gold set with garnet and lapis lazuli, incorporates elements of the Celtic style including the symbolic combination of centre, cross and circle. (Brooch from Kingston Down, Kent, England, 7th c. AD.)

45 The Celtic Revival of the nineteenth century, for all its Romantic emphasis and folksy zeal, succeeded in arousing a popular interest in our own ethnic poetry and literature. The real and unacknowledged work was done by thousands of patient educators like the two Welsh teachers, father and son, who designed this wall chart for Sunday-school children. (Y Wyddor, wall chart devised by T. C. Evans and drawn by Christopher Evans, Wales, 19th c.)

Y WYDDOR (The Alphabet)

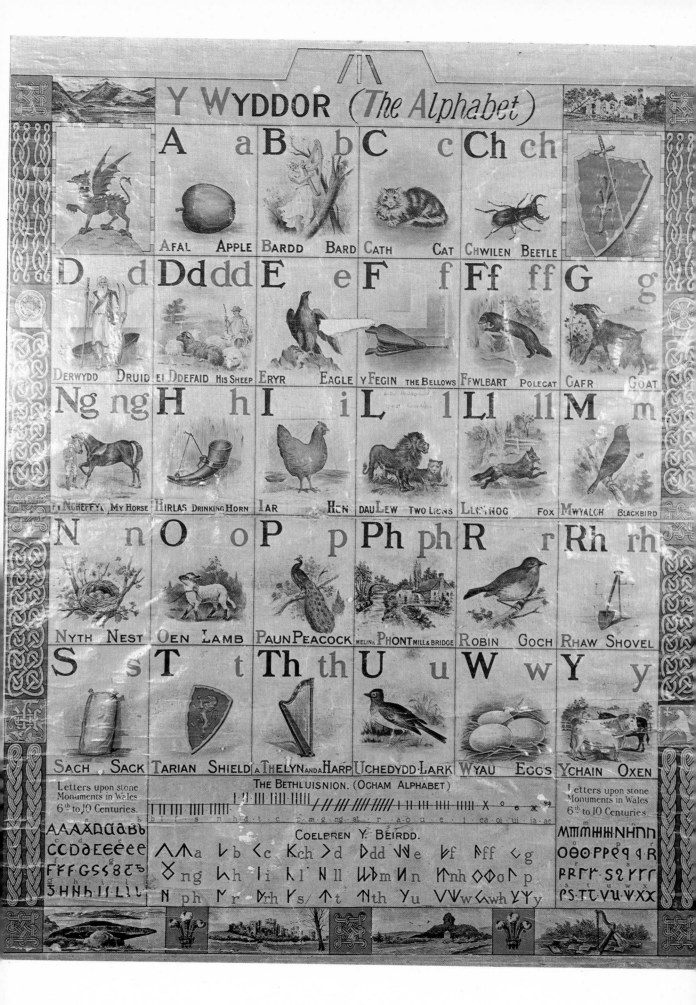

A a	B b	C c	Ch ch
AFAL APPLE	BARDD BARD	CATH CAT	CHWILEN BEETLE
D d	Dd dd	E e	F f	Ff ff	G g
DERWYDD DRUID	EI DDEFAID HIS SHEEP	ERYR EAGLE	Y FEGIN THE BELLOWS	FFWLBART POLECAT	GAFR GOAT
Ng ng	H h	I i	L l	Ll ll	M m
FY NGHEFFYL MY HORSE	HIRLAS DRINKING HORN	IAR HEN	DAU LEW TWO LIONS	LLWYNOG FOX	MWYALCH BLACKBIRD
N n	O o	P p	Ph ph	R r	Rh rh
NYTH NEST	OEN LAMB	PAUN PEACOCK	MELIN a PHONT MILL & BRIDGE	ROBIN GOCH	RHAW SHOVEL
S s	T t	Th th	U u	W w	Y y
SACH SACK	TARIAN SHIELD	A THELYN AND A HARP	UCHEDYDD LARK	WYAU EGGS	YCHAIN OXEN

THE BETHLUISNION. (OGHAM ALPHABET)

Letters upon stone Monuments in Wales 6th to 10 Centuries.

COELBREN Y BEIRDD.

Letters upon stone Monuments in Wales 6th to 10 Centuries

46, 47 A wooden door in a Cornish lane (left) conceals a well that has been sacred for at least a thousand years; and a Victorian well-cover, with Celtic Revival iron-work (below), covers the well on Chalice Hill beside Glastonbury Tor. The waters of this spring flow through a channel of chalybeate and are reputed to have healing properties. (46 St Ambrew's Well, Crantock, near Newquay, Cornwall, England; 47 The Chalice Well, Glastonbury, Somerset, England.)

48 Many holy wells and springs have been sacred from time immemorial. Despite outward changes in image and ritual, the act of invocation of the source of life has never wavered. This well was once sacred to the mother goddess Brigid, whose aspects of healing, fire and water were Christianized under the name of St Brigid, patron saint of hearth, home and sacred wells. (Well of St Brigid, Liscannor, Co. Clare, Ireland.)

*Documentary illustrations
and commentaries*

1 Stone relief from a holy well, showing triad of fertility goddesses, or Matronae, from Mümling-Grumbach, Odenwald,
Germany, Celto-Roman period. (see pls. 14, 48.)

2

3

N

0   50   100m

1
2

a

Tall menhir

x

c

w

b

Temples of the sky

For people dependent on the seasonal rhythms of the earth, the movements of the sun and moon were vital, and an eclipse was a moment of awesome significance. The mysterious sacred centres of Western Europe are linked in popular tradition, rightly, with the Druidic religion of the Celts. We now know that they were not built by the Celts, but date back to a far earlier civilization, the shadowy megalithic (or 'great stone') culture of the second and third millennia BC. However, what we know of the oral tradition of the Druids, whom a Greek writer called 'the originators of philosophy', suggests that they understood the astronomical significance now known to underlie such monuments as Stonehenge, Avebury (2), Carnac (3) and Callanish (4). These, and others such as Newgrange in Ireland and Maes Howe (11) in the Orkneys, have many features in common: a large man-made earth mound that was probably covered in layers of organic and inorganic material and faced with quartz, a great ditch, ceremonial causeways, numerous small burial mounds, a sacred well, a large henge of rough-hewn stones, and single monoliths. The largest of the monoliths, the Stone of the Fairies (Er Grah) at Carnac, now broken into four pieces, was 67 ft (nearly 21 m) long and weighed over 340 tons. Professor Thom has shown that these constructions, with their striking geometric pattern, were based on the megalithic yard (2.72 ft or 81.25 cm). By reconstructing the possible original layout of the Carnac alignments, using statistical analysis, he suggests that they were used for predicting eclipses, with Er Grah as a universal lunar foresight.

2 Avebury, near Stonehenge, Wiltshire, England, in prehistoric times. (Reconstruction drawing by Alan Sorrell.)

3 Alignments of the stones at Le Menec, Carnac, Morbihan, France. (A. Thom and A. S. Thom, 'The Carnac Alignments', *Journal for the History of Astronomy*, 1972.)

4 The small stone circle at Callanish, Lewis, Scotland, *c.* 2000–1500 BC.

4

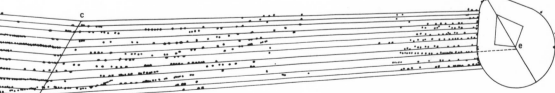

The inner quest

The tradition of vision, and the inner quest by the shaman, the Druid, the saint or the holy man, seem to be concentrated at specific places where the energy forces of the planet are located. The Celtic and pre-Celtic shaman, the living embodiment of the collective psyche, was the link with the ancestral spirit world. He performed the ceremonies connected with the dead, and the annual rites of renewal on behalf of the living. The age-old communal tomb which was the source of his power was the place where the forces of heaven and earth could meet. The vulva-shaped megalithic dolmens from Cornwall and India (5, 6) show how widespread was the ancient belief in the burial receptacle as a womb-place of the Earth Mother and the Other-world (see also pl. 14, pp. 78–79). These tombs were usually constructed with giant stone slabs forming a chamber and a trenched passageway, the gaps filled with dry-stone walling and covered by a great mound of earth. Dolmens, quoits and cromlechs are the remains of the original chambers. Natural caves and artificial chambers cut into the rock were also used.

The block of sandstone, 28 ft (8.6 m) long, which is called the Dwarfie Strane (8), is an example, unique in Britain, of a rock-cut chamber. It may have been used for meditation or initiation; for 'at each end is a bed and pillow of stone capable of holding two persons, with a hole above to admit light and allow smoke to escape'. The early Christian saints of Ireland and Scotland continued the tradition of using rock cavities for meditation and prayer. They chose mountains, islands and desolate places not only to avoid distraction but also to be closer to the Sacred. The church near Bilbao (7), actually built round a group of natural standing stones, and dedicated to St Michael, the dragon-slayer beloved of the Celts, is a remarkable example of the Christianization of a sacred place.

5 Chun Quoit, Cornwall, England.

6 Cromlech at Malabar, India. (Higgins, *The Celtic Druids*, London 1829.)

7 The dolmen of San Miguel, Arrichinaga, Spain, built into a church. (Fergusson, *Rude Stone Monuments*, London 1872.)

8 The Dwarfie Strane, rock-cut chamber on the Isle of Hoy, Orkney, Scotland.

9 Burial chamber with cairn at Bryn Celli Ddu, Anglesey, Wales, restored.

8

9

The spiral journey

Megalithic communal burial chambers have been found in Malta, Sicily, Southern France, Spain, Brittany, England, Ireland, Wales, Scotland, the Orkneys and around the Baltic. The shape alters with the location, from the beehive or tholos type of the south to the stone-boat burials of the north. The cutting of the massive slabs, and the similarity of construction over such a wide area, indicates a homogeneous pre-Celtic culture. Such undeniable evidence of technology, temple-based religion and spiral symbolism has created one of the oldest mysteries associated with the Celtic lands of the west (10).

Where the megalithic builders came from is an old issue of debate. The culture may have evolved locally in the British Isles; moved north-west from the Mediterranean in search of gold, tin and amber; or even spread eastwards from the submerging Atlantean civilization. Bristle-cone dating analysis has shown that the most outstanding stone temples in Malta and at Newgrange in Ireland, with their giant spiral capstones and corbelled stone roofing, were built over five thousand years ago. The information the builders left behind them, even in the burial chambers, is scanty in archaeological terms. However, their symbols are unmistakable. The curving loops of the great spiral (13, 14) show the journey of the soul moving through death to find rest and rebirth in the central chamber.

The only untouched passage grave in Western Europe that has been properly excavated was at Knowth in 1968 (12). Its contents were mainly large quantities of burnt bone – the remains of human cremations which had been washed completely white. These heaps were either placed on the floor, in stone basins or against the standing stones outside. Small objects such as stone balls, beads, miniature hammer pendants and bone pins with mushroom-shaped heads were also found.

Beneath a 24-ft-high (7.3 m) mound is the 15-ft-square (4.5 m) stone chamber at Maes Howe (11). The entrance passage is lined with slabs 18 ft (5.5 m) long. Both sides had a recess for placing the bodies inside. It remained sealed for about three thousand years until AD 1150, when Norse pirates broke in to spend a winter sheltering from the snow. They recorded their visit by carving a dragon and the message in runes that they had removed its treasure.

10 Interior of megalithic tomb at Viera, Spain.

11 Interior of burial chamber at Maes Howe, Orkney, Scotland, c. 2500–2000 BC.

12 Passage in tumulus at Knowth, Co. Meath, Ireland.

13, 14 Interior of main chamber of Gavrinis passage grave, Larmor-Barden, Morbihan, France.

10

11

78

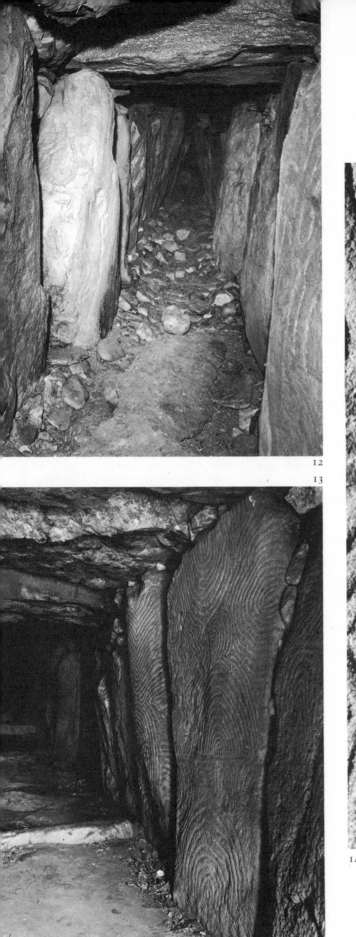

12

13

14

15

16

The primal energy

In Indian religious ceremonies the sexual nature of elemental stone is accorded full recognition in the lingam. Male and female energy properties are identified with the creative and beneficial sources of the universe. Tantric rites are thoroughly integrated into a comprehensive system of psychic liberation. On a different level, the ancient natural religion has always made a special feature of orgiastic rituals where the drama of positive and negative energy sources finds its focus in sexually shaped stones and totem-objects.

The standing stones from Corsica (19) are crude examples of the brute force associated with the phallus. The carved 'faces' on many of them heighten the analogy. The carving of basic patterns (18, 20), and the gradual shaping of the crude elemental force (21), took place over millennia, until the design itself became a symbol of power, as on the beautifully carved Pictish cross (22).

The extraordinary similarity between the Turoe stone (16), with its patterns of curving foliage in the La Tène manner, and the Navel of the World stone from Delphi (15), may be a clue to the cult significance of this and other round stones in Ireland. The worship of Pythia, the snake goddess of the Delphic Oracle, was suppressed by Apollo, who also changed the name and emphasized the prophetic and healing aspects of the sanctuary (which was to be sacked by the Celts in 279 BC).

19

20

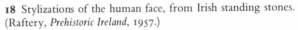

17 18

There are many references to the serpent (or dragon) in the Irish stories, and the most likely cult centre would have been the healing fire sanctuary of Brigid at Kildare.

15 The Navel of the World from Delphi, Greece. (Delphi Museum.)

16 The Turoe Stone, Ireland, late Iron Age.

17 Cast of the Castlestrange Stone at Castlestrange, Co. Roscommon, Ireland. (National Museum of Ireland, Dublin.)

18 Stylizations of the human face, from Irish standing stones. (Raftery, *Prehistoric Ireland*, 1957.)

19 Standing stones at Filitosa, Corsica.

20 Standing stone at Glencolumbcille, Co. Donegal, Ireland.

21 Cross on Skellig Michael, Co. Kerry, Ireland, 7th c. AD.

22 Pictish carved stone cross at the Manse, Glamis, Angus, Scotland, 8th c. AD.

21 22

The sacred well

The evidence of place-names and archaeology indicates that the main religious centres in Britain during the Roman period were concentrated around the Severn basin in the south-west, and near Hadrian's Wall in the north (23). The Hooded Ones (24), and their associations with fertility and healing, were known in both areas. The hood (*cochull*) is referred to in Irish mythology in connection with the Peaked Red One, a god of the Underworld.

The custom of hanging clooties on trees or bushes by a sacred well was once widespread throughout Scotland, Wales and Ireland (25). It is also common in the Middle East. The symbolism connected with the mother goddess has been largely forgotten since the change to church-based Christian ritual. However, the venerative force of water, which played an important part in the ancient Celtic religion (23), is still recognized in a few folk customs connected with holy wells.

23 Stone dedicated to the water goddess Coventina, from Carrawburgh, Northumberland, England, 2nd–3rd c. AD; see pl. 14. (Museum of Antiquities, Newcastle-upon-Tyne.)

24 Stone plaque dedicated to the Genii Cucullati, the Hooded Ones, from Housesteads, Northumberland, England, 3rd c. AD; see pl. 19. (Housesteads Museum.)

25 A holy well near Duncannon, Co. Wexford, Ireland.

26 Stone relief of Cernunnos, flanked by Apollo and Mercury, from Reims, Marne, France, 2nd c. AD. (Musée de Reims.)

27 Cave drawing from Val Camonica, Italy, c. 4th–3rd c. BC. (Ananti, *Camonica Valley*, London 1964; see pls. 24, 25.)

28 Relief of Cernunnos, Gallo-Roman. (Musée de Cluny, Paris.)

The Horned One

Celtic kingship rituals, as reflected in the Irish sagas, show the shaman in a trance state projecting the power of an animal archetype. The cave drawing of such a ritual (the horned figure wears the torc and serpent arm ornaments of Celtic iconography) has many affinities with world-wide representations of Palaeolithic shamanism (27). This stag god is one of the few early animal spirits for whom we have a name, known from a unique inscription: Cernunnos, the Horned One or the Lord of All the Stags (28). In Gallo-Roman art he became associated with Pan; note the rat which indicates his chthonic power (26). The bag of coins in his lap expresses his perennial function as a provider; he remained a god of prosperity and good fortune, as he had been for the early hunters.

Double- and triple-headed stone images (29, 30, 33), and the Tau cross (31), claimed as an old masonic symbol of the travelling stonemen, show the many-faced and all-pervading power of consciousness that was central to the Celtic perception of the world. The brooding earth-power is still evident in the Janus figure (29), with its stylized leaf-crown.

29 Stone Janus figure from Holzgerlingen, Württemberg, Germany, c. 6th–5th c. BC. (Landesmuseum, Stuttgart.)

30 Three-faced stone head from Corleck, Co. Cavan, Ireland, c. 3rd–2nd c. BC. (National Museum of Ireland, Dublin.)

31 Stone Tau cross, Killinaboy, Co. Clare, Ireland.

29

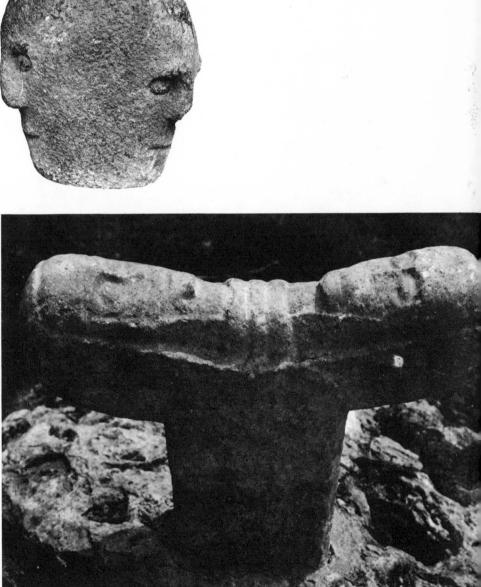

30

31

The eternal presence

The human head, as the centre of spiritual power, had overwhelming significance for all the Celtic peoples. It is conspicuous in their rituals, their warfare and their stories, and appears in their art from the earliest known representations in Central Europe to the illuminated manuscripts of the Christian Irish. The Celts were head-hunters, and there was more to their collection of these trophies than the desire to boast of their prowess. The use of real or man-made heads as decoration, in triads or various other combinations of sacred numbers (33, 34, 36, 37), reflects the protective power which was thought to reside in them. The Celts were dependent on the horse-drawn chariot for their survival and dominance, and the trophy head was a common emblem on such items as linchpins and harness (35, 36).

32 Standing stone at Filitosa, Corsica.

33 Three-faced urn from Carinthia, Austria, 3rd c. BC. (Landesmuseum, Klagenfurt.)

34 Gold bracelet in early La Tène style from Bad Dürkheim, near Neustadt, Palatinate, Germany, 1st millennium BC. (Historisches Museum der Pfalz, Speyer am Rhein.)

35 Silver horse trappings showing trophy heads and the triskele symbol of Manannán Mac Lir, from Manerbia sul Mella, Italy, 1st millennium BC. (See pl. 24.)

36 Iron and bronze linchpin from chariot-wheel, in late La Tène style, from Grabenstetten, Reutlingen, Germany, 4th–2nd c. BC. (Württembergisches Landesmuseum, Stuttgart.)

37 A reconstruction of the sanctuary at Roquepertuse, Bouches-du-Rhône, France, 3rd–2nd c. BC; see p. 28. (Musée Borely, Marseilles.)

32   33

34

35

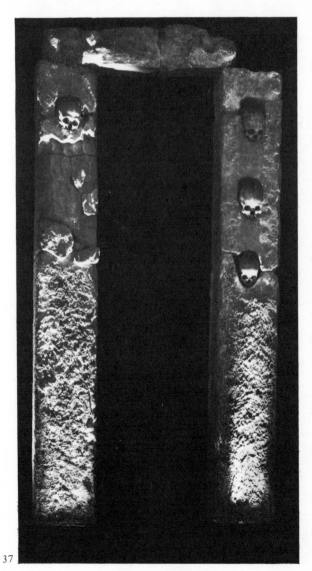

36

37

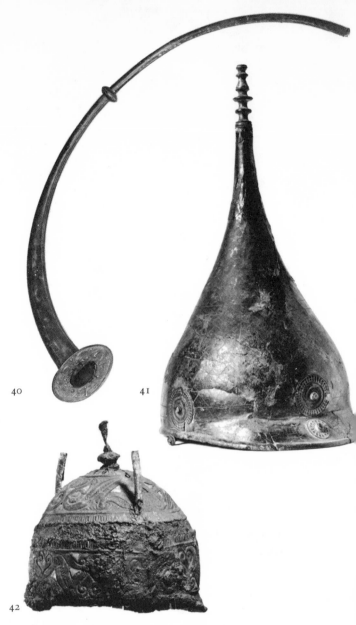

38

39   40   41

42

38 Gallic armour as Roman trophies of war, detail of relief on the Arc de Triomphe at Orange, Vaucluse, France, *c.* 1st c. AD.

39 Defeated Gaul, detail of a relief showing a battle between Romans and Gauls, Mausoleum of the Julii at Glanum, near Saint-Rémy de Provence, Bouches-du-Rhône, France, 1st c. AD; see pls. 29, 30. (Plateau des Antiques, Saint-Rémy dé Provence.)

40 Bronze trumpet from Lough-na-Shade, Co. Armagh, Ireland, 2nd–1st c. BC. (National Museum of Ireland, Dublin.)

41 Iron helmet with bronze and coral decoration from Canossa di Puglia, Italy, 4th c. BC. (Staatliche Museen Preussicher Kulturbesitz, Antikenabteilung, Berlin.)

42 Bronze helmet from a grave at La Gorge Meillet, Marne, France, 5th c. BC. (Musée des Antiquités Nationales, Saint-Germain-en-Laye.)

43 Bronze votive chariot from Strettweg, Styria, Austria, 7th c. BC. (Landesmuseum Joanneum, Graz.)

Warriors

The strut and delight of the Celtic warriors in ceremonial and war gear, their preoccupation with personal appearance, their ritualistic boasting, their indifference to death, were all part of the warrior mystique. When Alexander the Great asked what the Celtic Galatians feared, he was told: 'That the sky should fall.' This mystique was served by the skill of the smiths and other artisans, who provided the heroes with personal symbols of their power and prowess: thus, the sword was an honour bond and usually had (as in Arthurian legend) a pet name known only to its owner. Something of the splendour of Celtic armour decoration is known to us from a Roman victory arch showing the trophies of war (38); another image left to us by the triumphant enemies of the Gauls (39) is a reminder that the pick of the Celtic warriors scorned death by fighting naked, in a sacred frenzy in which life and death were as one.

Even in death, the Celtic warrior retained his finery: in Central and Northern Europe, he was laid on a four-wheeled wagon in a rock chamber and covered with a mound of earth. Many of these tombs have been found to contain elaborate weaponry and ornaments in iron and bronze, including swords, helmets (41, 42), war trumpets (40), torcs, amulets and harness. The bronze model (43) probably represents (and served as a substitute for) one such burial. It includes figures representing immolated retainers, weapons, includes warriors, horses, weapons and sacred beasts surrounding the figure of a goddess holding up the bowl of the sky.

43

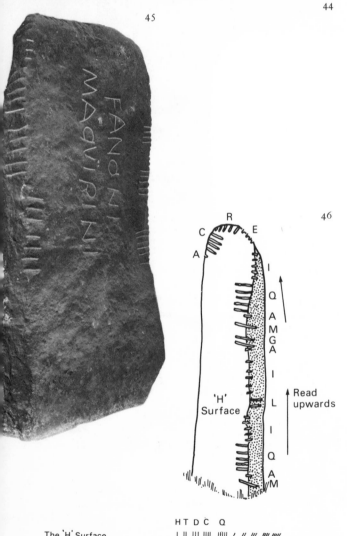

44

45

46

The act of naming

Language begins with the mark, with naming the unknowable. The primal act attempts to confine or alter the forces of nature within an order or pattern. The traditional Ogham alphabet was a simple progression of this principle, and ideal for incising both edges of a rough burial stone. Common in the south of Ireland (Macalister has found over 900 examples throughout the British Isles) and Scandinavia, its origins are obscure. Lucian's story of an old man in Gaul dressed in a lion's skin, with tiny gold chains tied to his tongue, representing Ogmios, is the only reference to such a Celtic god of knowledge and wisdom.

The Coligny calendar, unearthed in 1897 (44), shows how far the Romanization of Gaul had progressed by the first century AD. It was composed of about 60 bronze fragments, which when pieced together showed a table of 62 consecutive months of 30 auspicious or bright days and 29 inauspicious or dark days. It seems to have been an attempt to graft Roman ideas on to the Celtic thirty-six-month ritual cycle.

Within the realm of the eternal present which is reflected in Celtic myth and legend, the designation of good and bad days, or even of certain hours for brave deeds, was the prerogative of the Druid. The bards foretold the future from bird calls, from the paths of animals, and from casting yew sticks; divination was inseparable from the natural lore of the forest. The first three letters of the ancient Irish alphabet of the trees, Beth-Luis-Nion, correspond to the birch, the rowan and the ash. This succinct oral method of memorizing a wide range of knowledge was useful in herbal healing and other magical practices. A visual counterpart of this ancient tradition is the monogram page of the Book of Kells (47). Its dense, luxuriant world of hidden meanings, pictures and designs forms one of the most elaborate and beautiful examples of calligraphy in the Western world (48).

44 Detail of bronze plaque showing the Gallic calendar, from Coligny, Ain, France, 1st c. AD. (Musée Archéologique, Fourvière, Lyon.)

45 Stone with Ogham inscription and the names of two Irishmen, Suaqqucos and Fanonus, from Ivybridge, Devon, England, 6th c. AD. (British Museum, London.)

46 The Ogham alphabet, together with an example from the tomb of Maquiliaq son of Erca, in Co. Kerry, Ireland, 1st millennium AD. (Thomas, *Britain and Ireland in Early Christian Times*, London and New York 1971.)

47 Initial XPI (*Christi generatio*) from the Book of Kells, Ireland, 8th c. AD. (Trinity College, Dublin.)

48 Ornamented capitals from the Book of Kells. (Bain, *Celtic Art, the Methods of Construction*, reprinted London 1972.)

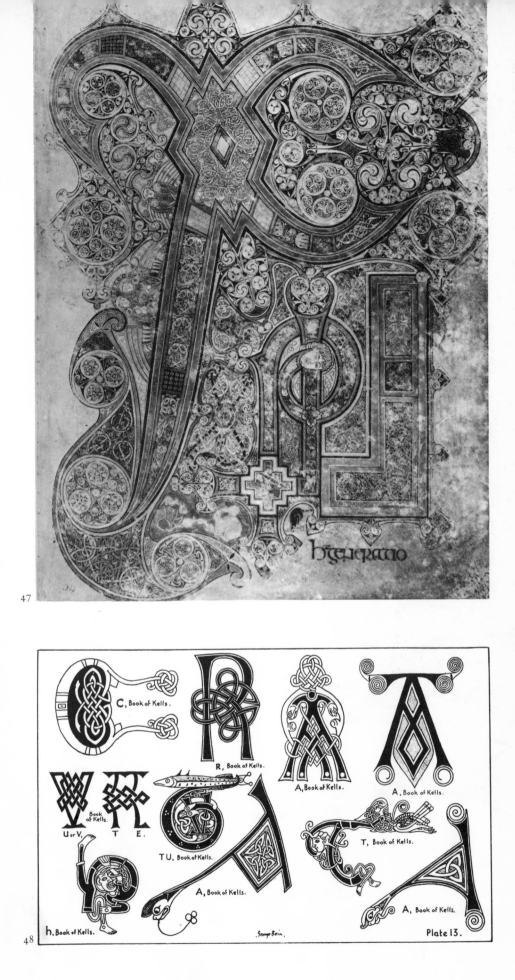

47

hЗeneratio

48   .Seerge Bain.   Plate 13.

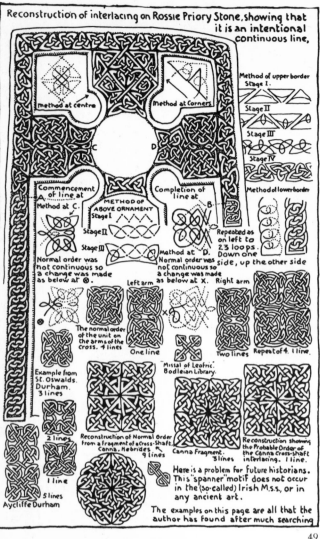

49

Intricate contemplation

Ireland was the only Celtic country to preserve the old ways of the heroic period, continuing into the Christian Middle Ages an artistic tradition formed over a thousand years before in the La Tène culture of Central Europe. Common design elements were the knot, the geometric interlace, and the punning use of multiple curved lines to generate shapes derived from plants, birds, animals and people – as in the man (52) who turns into a fish, a traditional symbol of Christ, and also of the soul. The same constant factors of style appear in the great Irish Gospel Books (those of Kells, Durrow, Lindisfarne and elsewhere) and in objects of devotion such as crosses (49, 53) and reliquaries (51).

It is a common practice among contemplatives to occupy the conscious mind with some demanding but repetitive task (a mantra or a rosary). The intricate Irish ornaments are aids to such concentration. The two beard-pullers, contemplating the knots of eternity – a recurrent image in the Book of Kells – are using a technique of paired meditation which has been revived, notably by encounter groups, in our own time (50).

49 Continuous lines of Celtic ornament. (Bain, *Celtic Art, the Methods of Construction*, reprinted London 1972.)

50 Beard-pullers from the Book of Kells. (Bain, *Celtic Art, the Methods of Construction*, reprinted London 1972.)

51 Irish shrine found in Norway, 8th–9th c. AD; see pl. 36. (Nationalmuseet, Copenhagen.)

52 Marginal ornament from the Book of Kells, Irish, 8th c. AD; see pl. 40. (Trinity College, Dublin.)

53 Ornamental knop with animal head, supporting the Cross of Cong; see pl. 37. (National Museum of Ireland, Dublin.)

50   51

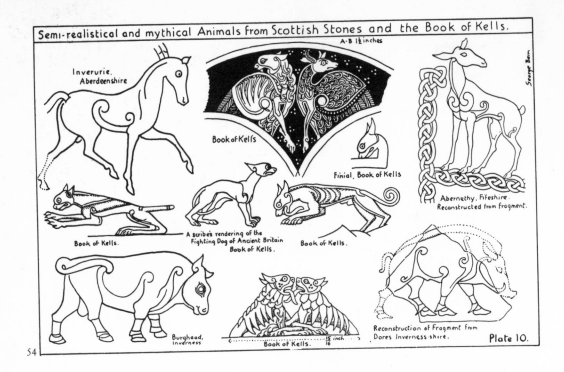

Semi-realistical and mythical Animals from Scottish Stones and the Book of Kells.

A·B 1½ inches

George Bain

Inverurie, Aberdeenshire

Book of Kells

Finial, Book of Kells

Abernethy, Fifeshire. Reconstructed from fragment.

Book of Kells.

A scribe's rendering of the Fighting Dog of Ancient Britain. Book of Kells.

Book of Kells.

Burghead, Inverness

Book of Kells.

15/16 inch

Reconstruction of Fragment from Dores Inverness-shire.

Plate 10.

54

The power of beasts

The art and literature of the Celts contains a rich bestiary, the most favoured animals being the stag, the bull, the boar and the horse. The psycho-sexual nature of the rituals involving shaman and animal – part of a very old Indo-European tradition – suggests that animals were identified with the ancestral spirit who presided over the fortunes of the tribe. The Lord of the Animals shown on the Sutton Hoo purse (55) is almost identical with the Cernunnos on the Gundestrup cauldron (pl. 24). The bull (58) was a beast of power to the pastoral British and Irish, as the stag and boar (57) were to huntsmen, the horse to the early nomadic Celts, and the prowling wolf to the wild Picts (58). The sacred nature of all these animals is reflected in the stories of shape-shifting and magic hunts in the Gaelic tales.

The work of George Bain (48, 49, 51, 54) deserves special mention. A craftsman as meticulous as any of those whose work he so lovingly studied, he spent a lifetime abstracting the major Celtic design motifs from manuscripts and stones, and showing how their extraordinarily unified symbolism was achieved; his work is nothing less than a guide to the Celtic world of the imagination.

55

54 Animal forms from Celtic art. (Bain, *Celtic Art, the Methods of Construction*, reprinted London 1972.)

55 Detail of the purse from the ship burial at Sutton Hoo, Suffolk, England, 7th c. AD. (British Museum, London.)

56 Bronze mount in the form of a bull, from Dorset, England, 1st c. AD. (Dorset County Museum, Dorchester.)

57 Bronze boar from Bata, Hungary, 1st c. BC–1st c. AD. (Magyar Nemzeti Múzeum, Budapest.)

58 Stone incised with figure of a wolf, from Ardross, Inverness-shire, Scotland, 7th c. AD; see pl. 42. (Inverness Museum.)

94

56

57

58

59

This unique pictographic stone, which has a sun symbol on its other face and ogham characters on one side, is now mounted upside-down on a concrete plinth in the British Museum. It can be seen as a map of the adventures of a local hero or chief, with a proliferation of symbols for boats, water and other objects; as such it has similarities with rock carvings found in North America and elsewhere. But it was more probably part of a capstone over the entrance to a burial chamber, depicting the voyage of the soul through different realms of consciousness.

59 Stone from Trecastle, Wales. (British Museum, London.)

Sources and further reading

Bord, Janet and Colin, *Mysterious Britain*, London 1972.
Castaneda, Carlos, *The Teachings of Don Juan*, Berkeley 1968.
Chadwick, Nora, *The Celts*, Harmondsworth 1970.
Chaplin, Dorothea, *Matter, Myth and Spirit*, London 1935.
Dillon, Myles, and Nora Chadwick, *The Celtic Realms*, London 1967.
Evans-Wentz, W.Y., *The Fairy Faith in Celtic Countries*, London 1911.
Graves, Robert, *The White Goddess*, London 1958.
Gregory, Lady, *The Voyages of St Brendan . . . A Book of Saints and Wonders*, Gerrards Cross 1973.
Henry, Françoise, *Irish Art*, London 1965.
Higgins, Geoffrey, *The Celtic Druids*, London 1829.
Jackson, Kenneth Hurlstone, *A Celtic Miscellany*, Harmondsworth 1971.
Jarman, A.O.H., *The Legend of Merlin*, Cardiff 1970.
Kinsella, Thomas (tr.), *The Táin*, Oxford 1969.
Macalister, R.A.S., *Tara, a Pagan Sanctuary*.
Mac Cana, Proinsias, *Celtic Mythology*, London 1970.
Menzies, Lucy, *St Columba of Iona*, Glasgow 1949.
Mercier, Vivian, *The Irish Comic Tradition*, Oxford 1962.
Rees, Alwyn and Brinley, *Celtic Heritage*, London 1961.
Ross, Anne, *Pagan Celtic Britain*, London 1967.
Sjoestedt, M.-L., *Gods and Heroes of the Celts*, London 1949.
Waters, Frank, *The Book of the Hopi*, New York 1969.